West Academic Publishing's Law School Advisory Board

a short & happy guide to

Copyright

Michael D. Murray
University of Massachusetts
School of Law

A SHORT & HAPPY GUIDE® SERIES

WEST
ACADEMIC
PUBLISHING

The publisher is not engaged in rendering legal or other professional advice, and this publication is not a substitute for the advice of an attorney. If you require legal or other expert advice, you should seek the services of a competent attorney or other professional.

a short & happy guide series is a trademark registered in the U.S. Patent and Trademark Office.

© 2017 LEG, Inc. d/b/a West Academic

    444 Cedar Street, Suite 700
    St. Paul, MN 55101
    1-877-888-1330

Printed in the United States of America

ISBN: 978-1-68328-940-1

About the Author

Professor Michael Murray currently teaches at the University of Massachusetts School of Law. He previously taught at the University of Kentucky College of Law, the University of Michigan Law School, Valparaiso University School of Law, the University of San Diego School of Law (in Florence, Italy), the University of Illinois College of Law, and Saint Louis University School of Law. He practiced law at Bryan Cave LLP law firm after clerking for U.S. District Judge John F. Nangle in the Eastern District of Missouri. Professor Murray graduated from Columbia Law School (JD, Harlan Fiske Stone Scholar), Loyola University—Maryland (BA, summa cum laude, Whelan Medal), and from Fudan University—Shanghai (Grad. Cert.).

Professor Murray is a busy scholar in the areas of copyright, trademark, right of publicity, and many other art law topics. In addition to his law review and journal articles, he is the author or co-author of ART LAW IN A NUTSHELL (West Academic); RIGHT OF PUBLICITY IN A NUTSHELL (forthcoming, West Academic); ART LAW DESKBOOK: ARTISTS' RIGHTS IN INTELLECTUAL PROPERTY, MORAL RIGHTS, AND FREEDOM OF EXPRESSION; FIRST AMENDMENT AND CENSORSHIP; THE DESKBOOK OF ART LAW; and ART LAW: CASES AND MATERIALS. He also is the co-author of the LRW Series of books at West Academic-Foundation Press, whose recent titles include ADVANCED LEGAL WRITING AND ORAL ADVOCACY: TRIALS, APPEALS, AND MOOT COURT 2D; LEGAL RESEARCH METHODS 2D; and LEGAL WRITING AND ANALYSIS 2D.

Table of Contents

A Short & Happy Guide to Copyright

Introduction

Copyright Law

All lawyers can benefit from a basic understanding of copyright law. Modern law practice strives to provide services and answer client needs across a growing variety of areas of commerce and law. Firms strive to be a one-stop solution for all of their clients' needs. And in these time of growing reliance on technology, big data, visual and audio media, and digital communication, clients of all types and sizes continue to develop legal needs in areas in that are affected by copyright law.

Lawyers exploring the modern legal landscape will find that many areas of commerce, science and technology, literature, entertainment, and the arts depend on lawyers who have more than a passing understanding of copyright law. The interest and attention we pay to creative, entertainment, and intellectual business matters raises the profile of legal problems that affect people who work and do business in these areas. Even focusing on one area—the arts and entertainment industry—reveals that artists, media companies, internet companies, publishing businesses, museums and galleries, insurers, government regulators, everyday consumers, and creative users and re-users of content encounter copyright issues on a daily basis. As a result, no knowledge of copyright law will go to waste in a lawyer's practice. Fortunately, although learning one more area of the law is never easy for the young lawyer starting out in practice, with copyright law the study need not be a burden, because copyright law is a fun and fascinating subject for study. This guide was written to help you start the journey.

If you are a law student purchasing this guide, you obviously are interested in the legal issues that arise in copyright law, the laws and legal standards that apply to answer the issues, and the information needed to make predictions about probable outcomes of copyright disputes. If you are a practitioner seeking to expand your knowledge with the hopes of expanding your practice, you have come to realize that a good portion of your existing or potential clients will continue to have questions that implicate copyright law. If you are simply curious to learn more about this field, read on with the assurance that no matter what your level of interest and experience, this guide is written with the assumption that you most likely do not have any prior knowledge about American intellectual property law or copyright law in particular. You need not even know that much about the law to pick up the ideas and concepts of this area. This is an open guide for the curious.

Using the Guide

The purpose of this guide is to orient and acclimate you to the structure, public policy, issues, and vocabulary of the area of copyright law. If you are using this guide while taking a copyright or intellectual property survey course, you will immediately recognize that a guide of this size cannot replace your course text and the supplemental materials assigned by your professor. But it is worth your time to use this guide in the following ways:

- To get up to speed on the biggest issues of copyright law, and the black letter law addressing those issues, so as to help you master this area for your copyright, art law, or intellectual property survey course.

- To educate yourself as to your future clients' rights, potential liabilities, and options and opportunities regarding legal problems in copyright. Whether you plan to specialize in copyright or intellectual property, or simply want to be available to your firm or law office as an attorney who can take on a novel problem in an exciting and potentially high-profile and high-dollar-value area of your firm's or office's practice, this book will be useful to you. In many instances, copyright law has defined rights and responsibilities and created options and opportunities that are not known or fully understood by the average lawyer.

- To provide a vocabulary of legal terms to use when consulting with lawyers, clients, accountants, financial planners, and insurers regarding problems in the creative, entertainment, and scientific fields. When you find yourself involved in a matter that turns out to have copyright implications, this vocabulary will help you to be an active and helpful member of the team. It will help you to research, understand, and process the information you will need to give advice to the client and recommendations to your associates and superiors.

- To identify existing or potential legal problems in your client's and your organization's practices. This guide will discuss a variety of areas in which exposure to legal liability or sanctions may present itself as a current or future problem based on your clients' practices and procedures.

If your interest is piqued by this book, I suggest for further reading the texts from which many of the examples and illustrations throughout this book were drawn: 1 LEONARD D. DUBOFF, MICHAEL D. MURRAY, ET AL., ART LAW DESKBOOK: ARTISTS' RIGHTS IN INTELLECTUAL PROPERTY, MORAL RIGHTS, AND FREEDOM OF EXPRESSION, ch. 1 (2017), and LEONARD D. DUBOFF & MICHAEL D. MURRAY, ART LAW: CASES AND MATERIALS, ch. 2 (2d ed. 2017). These texts discuss the issues and problems in more detail, and discuss additional issues of art law that arise along with copyright issues. If your time or interest level is more modest, a general introduction to art law is provided in LEONARD D. DUBOFF, CHRISTY A. KING, & MICHAEL D. MURRAY, ART LAW IN A NUTSHELL (West Academic, 5th ed. 2017).

Welcome to the study of copyright law!

CHAPTER 1

Copyright Basics

Copyright is a wonderful, complex, sometimes mysterious area of law. In my experience as a law professor and legal author, I have encountered many students with a strong desire to learn something of copyright law. Many of you might plan to work with media giants and entertainment companies. You might want to work with producers of motion pictures and television programming, and with online content providers. You would be happy to represent artists, authors, publishers, and persons consuming or re-using content. You also would like to be useful to your firm and its clients regarding copyright protection for your clients' products and works well beyond the arts and entertainment fields. Copyright law addresses all of these questions and curiosities. We will begin with some basic issues.

An Author

Right off the bat, you need to understand a term of art in copyright law: an **author**. Copyright law uses the term "author" to mean anyone who creates things in expressive media. So, author can be used to mean artist, composer, playwright, photographer, cinematographer, or musician, or a publisher who publishes, sells, and distributes creative works (and owns the copyright to the works). It can mean a scientist who writes reports of her findings and generates charts and diagrams. It can mean a computer programmer (coder) who produces works in a computer language of source code and object code for the express purpose of communicating a result in that computer language. It can mean a business that creates a new visual or auditory design for cloth, textiles, flooring, toys, or other products. Many of the examples in this book come from the visual arts, so I often will use the term **"artist"** as interchangeable with author.

The Work

I mentioned author. Now, let's learn the word **"work."** The work is that thing which the author creates. It is that simple. I mentioned a huge, open-ended list of the possible activities and professions of copyright authors, and so it goes with the variety of works that may be subject to copyright protection. Anything that is expressive and created by an author may be protected by copyright.

The term "work" is not reflective of a certain level of effort, although the work must be "authored," which you will learn means conceived of in the mind of the author and then created in a form in which the work can be perceived. The "conception" part is as important as the "creation" part. Happy accidents not conceived of and not brought into existence by a deliberate act of the author do not count as works. Things already in existence, and not brought into existence by an author do not count. But the law does not require any particular level of effort or "work" for a work to qualify as a work.

Note, too, that the "work" is not the subject matter of the work. Many artists can paint the same person, the same scene, or the same objects, and each will have created a separate work—unless one of them copies the work of another. If copying is present, we have a genuine problem under copyright law, not because of the common subject matter, but because of the copying.

Obtaining a Copyright

Getting a copyright is not complicated. All you need to do is write something, paint something—do something that creates something. Copyright protects works in every expressive media, and even media in which it is hard to appreciate what has been created without the aid of a machine or other device, such as in the source code of a computer program. Writings, paintings, drawings, musical compositions and musical recordings, literature, plays, poems, motion pictures, pantomimes, and computer programs are copyrightable once the author finishes them.

Expression and Fixation in Media

The formal parts (meaning, parts that relate to the form of the work) that matter to copyright are: **Expression** and **Fixation in Media**. "Expression" means the work has to have some communicative potential for one of the senses. What must you be trying to communicate?—It really doesn't matter, just communicate something, anything. Communicate the idea of something. Copyright is broad. It only is looking for an author to communicate a concept that can exist as an idea in the mind of the author and be communicated to the mind of someone else through some communicative media. And "fixation in media" means that it has to be in some form in which it can be perceived by one of the senses for long enough that other people can tell what the creation is and receive its communication. The law defines "fixation" as:

> authorship fixed in any tangible medium of expression, now known or later developed, from which [the works] can be perceived, reproduced, or otherwise

communicated, either directly or with the aid of a machine or device.[1]

If you conceive of a work, and fix it in some perceptible media so that it can communicate your conception to others, then you've got a copyright over that work—whatever it is you created.

Registering Your Copyright Is Not Required

No registration is required. If you heard something different, console yourself with the fact that United States copyright law used to require registration. The law changed when the United States passed its latest, massive copyright overhaul, the Copyright Act of 1976. After this, in the early 1980's, the United States actively aligned its copyright law with the copyright laws of most of the rest of the nations of this world, who govern themselves according to the international copyright rules found in the Berne Convention. The Berne Convention does not require registration of copyrights, so now, neither does U.S. law.

I have to backtrack a little bit and say that registration is required if you want to sue someone over a copyright in a United States federal court. And that is an important thing to remember, because you cannot sue anyone over a copyright dispute in a state court. You just can't. Copyright law is federal law. There is no such thing as state copyright law, and state courts have no power (no jurisdiction) to hear any suit involving copyright law. Students studying jurisdiction in civil procedure and constitutional law should know that copyright is an area of complete federal preemption (for the rest of you, you can just smile and nod). For our purposes here, it's federal court or nothing, and for that, you have to register your copyright.

That doesn't mean you need to run to the Library of Congress website, www.loc.gov, right now and register all of your works. It is fine to wait until you see someone copying one of your works, then register that work, and then sue the copyist. Or perhaps you register the work, then you or your lawyer write the copyist a cease and desist letter warning him that you believe he is violating your copyright, and then you sue him. You do get another special benefit when you register: you can sue for what is called "statutory damages" which you can recover from anyone who copies your works after you have registered them, and these damages are preset amounts that are generous. It beats having to prove actual damages—take my word for it.

Publication of the Work Is Not Required

No publication is required. Showing a work off to the world is called "publishing" or "publication," no matter if it is literature, printed work, a work of visual art, or something in an auditory or audio-visual media. Publication in the old copyright law sense meant registration with the Library of Congress, and it used to be a requirement of the law. It was coupled with a protection that only you, the author and creator, would have the right to make the first publication of the work. Now, publication no longer is a requirement because it isn't a requirement under the Berne Convention. You can write a novel or paint a picture and lock it away in a chest and never show it to anyone, and you still have a copyright over it. (Now, how is someone going to copy that, you ask? They can't, but don't get ahead of me. We are just going over some basics now!).

A Copyright Notice Is Not Required

Most people who have ever looked at the small print on a book or video have seen the "© 2017 Author B. Artist, All Rights Reserved" logo printed there. In spite of the ubiquity of this practice, the law currently provides that no copyright notice is required on copyrighted goods. It was required in the past, but the law changed to comply with the Berne Convention. Before the change in the law, showing the work to the world without having a copyright notice was the equivalent of donating it to the public domain where anyone could take it, copy it, and use it as they saw fit. But no more.

But there is a reason why authors and copyright owners still use the logo, "© year Author Name," and it is a good reason: if you use the notice, you will get protection from a potential infringer who might claim, "I didn't have any idea that that the work was copyrighted." True, that's not a defense that works every time—it is a little like the criminal defendant who swears to the judge, "I had no idea that armed robbery was illegal." But in certain circumstances the defense of innocent infringement does mitigate the copyright defendant's damages, and you can avoid that reduction in damages if you put a copyright notice on your work. You don't have to register the work before you put on the copyright notice; the copyright itself attaches at the moment you determine the work to be completed.

The "All Rights Reserved" part is added to the notice to comply with an international agreement called the Pan-American Copyright Treaty that still applies to countries in North and South America, including the United States. Although the Berne Convention affects many more countries than the Pan-American treaty, use of the "All Rights Reserved" logo may help you get relief for an infringement occurring in one of the North or South American countries still adhering to the Pan-American treaty.

Question: What Does Copyright Prevent? Answer: Copying

Copyright prevents copying. I don't mean to be flip or a smart aleck when I say this. It matters a great deal in copyright issues that there be an actual act of copying. If two works of expressive media look or sound quite a bit like each other, there always are two possible explanations: Some person copied the other person's work, or the two worked independently and just so happened to come up with something that looks or sounds similar. In copyright law, we call these two possibilities: **Copying** and **Random Independent Creation.**

Copying vs. Random Independent Creation

If you are a diligent and productive artist or author, and you work hard each day coming up with good, expressive works, and you look around and see other people producing good, expressive works that don't resemble yours, copyright law need not enter your mind. The creative works of others that don't resemble yours are no threat to you, except perhaps in a business or artistic competition sense. You can appreciate the abundance of creative works out there in the world, and not put a copyright lawyer in your phone's contacts list. All is well.

A trick to prove copying

Cartographers faced a recurring copyright problem in that they and their competitors were making maps of the same locations, and the locations were real life, naturally occurring, facts of the world. Therefore, a competitor might copy the map of another and claim—"No, I didn't copy. We just mapped the same place. We're both good map makers. Of course they look the same." Some cartographers resorted to putting coats of arms and portraits and text on their maps, as shown above, but this still didn't address the risk of the map itself being copied. Cartographers resolved the issue by creating small errors in the map—geographical anomalies that didn't exist in the real world. Then, if another cartographer copied the map and the error showed up, it was proof of copying—"That inlet doesn't exist in the real location!"

But then one day, you see someone displaying a work of expressive media that looks a whole lot like one of your works of expressive media. You say, "You copied me!" But the next thing out of the other person's mouth is, "No, I did not copy you. It is a case of random independent creation." This impasse is resolved in the law by answering a series of questions to try to figure out if the case is more likely to involve copying or some other explanation such as random independent creation:

Is There Evidence of Direct Copying?

If you are even slightly familiar with the law and how it works, you will not be surprised to learn that direct evidence of copying is rare. Suits are proved with indirect evidence or circumstantial evidence that makes the finding that someone copied someone else more likely than not. But once in a while, an artist is caught in the act, or leaves a paper trial with admissions about copying another work. And sometimes people will just be open and "honest" about their own copying and will freely admit to it. Usually these people think they can get away with it because they have a potential fair use (fair use means a person has a right to copy a work or part of a work without seeking permission; we'll get to that topic in Chapter 9). When these people admit it—"I copied."—that saves a lot of trouble not having to prove the act of copying. But don't get your hopes up. You won't always have this kind of evidence of copying, and in fact, usually it is quite rare. There are too few hidden cameras around, and the cheat doesn't fess up. If it appears that you don't have proof of actual copying, the alleged copyist doesn't admit it, and you didn't catch him in the act—then we ask:

Where and How Was the Original Work Published?

The point of this inquiry into where your own work was published is to try to figure out how likely it is that the alleged copyist would have had access to the work. Access, like copying, can be proved directly or indirectly. You may have proof of actual access: Did you work with this person? Were you their professor or supervisor? Did you have some reason to send your work to this person as a business proposal, a submission for a gallery, an entry in an art show, a screenwriting contest, or as a project in school? Other means of proof of access are more indirect, asking whether it is more likely than not that the person could have accessed the work: Was the work published in a magazine that the copyist subscribes to? Was it featured in a gallery show, and you have proof that the person attended that show? Was it at least posted on the internet, and this person had regular internet access? You and your lawyer will try to get creative answering this and the other questions, and will try to stack up the potentialities that this person had lots of opportunities to see your work. Next we ask:

How Similar Are the Two Works?

We consider similarity because if the two works are extremely similar—remarkably, strikingly similar—this can make up for poor evidence that the other person had access to your work. On the other hand, if the works are not very similar, you might be wasting your time with the suit.

The bottom line is, copying or random independent creation is a real possibility in every situation, and you have to spend time and money to rebut the latter, except in those delightful situations where the defendant simply admits it, "Oh yes, I copied it."

Who or What Is a Copyist?

We already broke into the topic of copying, so we must learn another copyright term of art: a copyist. A copyist is a term for a person who copies. We could say, "copier," but that term usually refers to a machine that makes photocopies these days. Copyist avoids that confusion. It is wrong to call the person a "plagiarist" or "infringer" at this stage because these terms are conclusions about the person's guilt or liability—an infringer improperly and unlawfully copied the work of another, and a plagiarist improperly passed off someone's work as her own. A copyist may well turn out to be an infringer or plagiarist, but we have to work to prove that these other titles fit.

The Basic Public Policy of Copyright Law

Copyright law, like any other significant topic of the law, is driven by a fundamental public policy. In the case of copyright, there are choices of whose or what interests should be championed in the law: the general public's interests and well-being, the personal interests of authors, the commercial interests of those who own or control copyrights, or some other more specific interest, such as the support of art, culture, history, or education. To find the answer, read the United States Constitution, Article I, section 8, clause 8, which states that copyright (and patent) law is intended:

> To promote the Progress of Science and useful Arts, by securing for limited Times to Authors and Inventors the exclusive Right to their respective Writings and Discoveries.

Thus, while authors (meaning, of course, content-creators of all varieties) seek intellectual property law protection as a way to protect their very livelihood, the public policy of the government is to enact and enforce intellectual property laws as a way to enrich and improve the lives of members of the general public. If you notice that the two aims are not directly connected, that is the beginning of the understanding of the definition and scope of coverage of the intellectual property laws, including copyright. The American intellectual property system is not an artist-incentive, or artist-reward based system. It is a public-oriented, public benefit system. So, the laws define and protect the subjects of protection with an eye to what best benefits the public at large, not what seems best to help artists live, thrive, and survive.

The Limits on Copyright's Protection

Copyright does not prevent all copying. I already mentioned fair uses—which in general involve copying an earlier work and reusing it or repurposing it in a manner that benefits the public. Remember that public policy we just looked at above? Copyright exists to benefit the public first, and the author second, and if not enforcing a copyright benefits the public in a way that at least matches the benefit of protecting the author and preventing the copying, then the act of unauthorized copying will be allowed. Fair uses will be covered in Chapter 9. But they are not the only limitation on copyright.

The Copyright Act, Title 17 of the United States Code, section 102(b)[2] states,

> In no case does copyright protection . . . extend to any idea, procedure, process, system, method of operation, concept, principle, or discovery, regardless of the form in which it is described, explained, illustrated, or embodied in such work.

This is a long list of things not covered because, once again, copyright law is a public policy driven set of laws, and the policy is: benefit the general public. Ideas and concepts can be copied, mimicked, emulated, and appropriated because the freedom to do those things improves the general welfare. It expands the topics of discussion by allowing people to think and express their thoughts on all manner of topics without the fear that you are repeating ideas and concepts that someone else has already thought about and talked about. Processes, procedures, methods, and recipes are not subject to copyright because they are useful, they benefit many members of society beyond the author, and the law wants them to be repeated and republished without the limitations of copyright. The term of copyright protection is long—the lifetime of the author and seventy more years after her death is the copyright term for a copyright owned and controlled by the author herself—and the law does not want good ideas to be locked up in the monopoly of copyright for that length of time. In addition, discoveries and inventions are not the stuff of copyright; we have patent law to protect truly inventive, innovative, and useful ideas, processes, inventions, and discoveries. Patent law has strict requirements, and only locks up the information for twenty years.

Although the exclusions are significant, copyright is a very important intellectual property protection: copyright protects *expressions* of ideas; communication of concepts; writings, descriptions, and depictions of processes, procedures, and methods. It protects the communicative form you create, in your own wording, arrangement, or depiction. It prevents others from copying *your* particular wording, arrangement, or depiction of the expressions (the works) you create. This distinction is call the "Idea-Expression Distinction," and it is the topic of Chapter 3 below.

Copyright Law Is the Same Throughout the United States

Copyright law is federal law that applies across the United States, in every state. The law does not vary from state to state, although some federal judges might interpret and apply the law a little differently, so the outcomes in cases might vary from circuit to circuit, and court to court.

---

[1]   17 U.S.C. § 101.

[2]   17 U.S.C. § 102.

CHAPTER 2

Originality and Creativity

The **formal** requirements of copyright were expression fixed in a tangible medium. Copyright also has two basic **conceptual** requirements:

(1) original

(2) creations

I could write these two conceptual requirements in a more typical copyright law phrasing: the "originality" requirement, and the "creativity" requirement. However, although accurate, using the words "originality" and "creativity" does not bring clarity to the concept of what copyright law requires, and in fact leads to confusion among lawyers, judges, clients, and laypersons. I don't mean a small amount of confusion; I mean fundamental confusion that leads to poor lawyering and bad judicial decisions. Therefore, I will break down these concepts carefully so as to set you off on the correct path to understanding.

First, know that all of these terms, original and originality, creation and creativity, are legal terms of art, meaning they don't mean exactly what you might expect them to mean. In copyright law, **original** means one thing: **not copied**. It does not mean unique, clever, ingenious, or inventive. It only means that the work originates with the author, and is not copied from another author's work. And **creation** means that the author created the work as a conception and work of the mind that is then produced and fixed by the author in some observable, perceptible media. Creation, creative, or creativity in copyright law also do not mean unique, clever, ingenious, or inventive. Creative means "**created by the author**," not found, not borrowed, and not naturally occurring.

A quick review of our other vocabulary so far might help: We have learned that the **work** protected by copyright is not the subject matter of the writing, painting, or photograph, or the ideas communicated by the work. The work is the composition, wording, arrangement, or depiction conceived of and created by the **author**. It is the expression of the subject matter that counts, not the actual ideas or subjects expressed and communicated. The **author** is the person who created the work. Whatever the work in question is, whatever the author's title, job description, training, or role is, the minimum broad requirement is that the author is the one who conceived of the work in her mind and brought it into existence herself, without copying it from another work.

What these concepts taken together mean is that the author must think up and create the work without taking or copying it from some other thing, including the work of another author. Things found in nature are not included—the author didn't think these up and didn't create them. The author can conceive of a way to arrange and depict naturally occurring or already existing things, but then the work protected only is the expression of the subjects as conceived of and depicted by the author. Other authors can take the same subject matter and think of their own way of writing it up or arranging and depicting the subjects, and receive copyright protection for their own original, creative expression of the subjects. We can unpack these concepts further with several examples:

A Painting as an Original, Creative Work

Consider the following painting of Brookings Hall of Washington University in St. Louis:[1]

What does the copyright to the painting protect? Not Brookings Hall itself. Not the appearance of Brookings Hall. Neither of those things was conceived of and created by the artist. Not even the idea of painting Brookings Hall in this particular perspective with the sun shining on it on a partly cloudy day is protected; ideas such as these are not protected in copyright. What is protected is this artist's own expression—rendered in paint—which represents the artist's conception of how he wanted to depict Brookings Hall, and which was created into existence by painting the conception of the mind into the physical expression shown here. It is this particular expression of the artist's conception of how to depict the hall that is protected.

This work has the two formal requirements of (1) expression (this expression is communicated visually), and (2) fixed in a tangible medium, and it has the two conceptual requirements of (3) an original work, that is not copied, (4) that was conceived of in the mind of the artist and created by the artist. Therefore, with these four requirements in place, the work is copyrightable and the artist possesses a copyright over this painting. The limits of this copyright are equally evident; anyone else can go to St. Louis and paint Brookings Hall, from this face-on perspective, even in direct sunlight on a partly cloudy summer day. But the second person cannot copy this artist's or any other artist's expression of the appearance of the hall.

Photographs as Original, Creative Works

The next example moves on to consider photographs. The image above is, of course, not a painting but a digital photograph depicting a painting. Is the photograph of the painting original and creative enough to obtain separate copyright protection?

In the past, the copyrightability of photographs was not a foregone conclusion. In the mid-nineteenth century, ambrotypists and daguerreotypists (early photographers) were not characterized as artists, and their works were not eligible for copyright protection. In 1865, Congress wrote photographs into the list of items that could potentially be copyrighted in the United States, but still the usefulness of this inclusion was illusory. Courts were reluctant to recognize photography as a copyrightable art form because they viewed photography as a purely mechanical production that took objects in the world and exposed the objects to a photo-chemical plate that reproduced the appearance of the objects fairly and accurately in all their features created by God or Mother Nature. That last phrase is the kicker: created by God or Mother Nature—not created by the artist. What was left for copyright? What could the photographer bring to a photograph that would look like an original conception of the mind that was created in a fixed and tangible form by the photographer?

The answer eventually came when courts gained a better understanding of the role and action of the photographer. Photographers create photos in every sense of the word. Whatever expression a photograph possesses is present because the photographer (the artist) put it there. The process of photography usually is not as time-consuming as painting or drawing, and in contemporary times, the entry-level skills required to get good results from photography are less than those required for getting good results from painting, drawing, and other visual arts. Many amateurs are happy to practice photography without any training or study. But the photographer creates the work nonetheless by processes of conception, composition, framing, cropping, controlling light levels, color, balance, saturation, focus, rendition, and many other active and creative processes. The necessary recognition for copyright is that the photograph is not naturally occurring, and it requires the intervention of an artist to use a tool (a camera) to create a work conceived of in the mind of the artist, perhaps in a split-second, and then created into existence by the voluntary act of the artist using the camera.

The courts slowly made their way to this realization: in 1884, in a case called *Burrows-Giles Lithographic Company v. Sarony*,[2] the United States Supreme Court evaluated the copyright claims of a photographer, Napoleon Sarony, who had created and photographed an entire scene featuring the writer, Oscar Wilde, who was on a tour of America. Sarony took great pains to arrange the writer on a certain couch, with a book in his hand, leaning forward, sitting on fur and tapestry drapery, with a floral backdrop, all of which he set up in his studio. The result was the photograph, "Oscar Wilde No. 18."

Oscar Wilde No. 18

Burrows-Giles Lithographic Company thought this photo was so nice that they made and sold 85,000 unauthorized copies of the image to be used for advertising of Mr. Wilde's stops across the country. Sarony, missing out on this apparently lucrative venture, sued for infringement of copyright. The lithographic company defended on the grounds that copyright couldn't control the reproduction of an image of Oscar Wilde, a living breathing entity of the world. Sarony didn't create the appearance of Oscar Wilde. All that mattered in their lithographic copies was the appearance of Oscar Wilde. You cannot have a copyright monopoly on images of Oscar Wilde, they argued.

The lithographers were right about that one thing: you cannot monopolize images of Oscar Wilde.

You can make your own depiction of Oscar Wilde, but you cannot copy someone else's depiction of Oscar Wilde. The idea of depicting Oscar Wilde, as well as Oscar himself, is free subject matter as far as copyright is concerned. Once someone actually creates a depiction (an expression) of Oscar, that particular depiction may not be copied without the permission of the creator of that depiction. That is what copyright prevents.

Anyone is free to make their own image of Oscar Wilde using a camera, or a pencil and paper, or paints and canvas. But Sarony didn't want to prevent the creation of all possible depictions of Wilde, he just wanted to protect *his* depiction of Wilde. In this case, the Supreme Court recognized Sarony's claim and ruled that the usurper could not copy Sarony's image of Oscar Wilde. Copyright protected the image, and the copying was held to be an infringement of the photograph.

The Supreme Court broke new ground in this case by recognizing that the expression of the photograph largely was conceived of and produced by Sarony—it was a work of his mind put down in the media of photographic paper. Sarony created the depiction—he brought his skills and artistic sensibilities to work to compose, arrange, stage, and produce the scene. The Supreme Court recognized that photographs created and produced in a manner similar to that of Sarony's could be original, creative works of art protectable by copyright.

What does that tell us about the photograph of the painting of Brookings Hall above—is it separately copyrightable? The answer is yes. Although in large part the photograph reproduces (copies) the appearance of the painting, and thus is not entirely "original" in its conception and expression, the photograph does crop and frame a portion of the original painting, and the cropping and framing performed could be protected by copyright. Not the entire photograph, because a large portion of the expression of that work is the original painting that is copied, but the particular cropping and framing conceived of and created by the artist can be protected.

Snap Shots as Original, Creative Works

The *Burrows-Giles* case allowed the copyrights of staged, studio photographs to be protected. But a question remained as to whether *all* photographs would be copyrightable, including snap shots. Snap shots, as the name implies, are taken very quickly. It does not always appear that the "conception of the mind" part is present. Here are some snap shots from my phone:[3]

Now here are some "snap shots" taken by the famous photographer, Alfred Stieglitz:[4]

Under current law, all of these snap shots are copyrightable works of art. The copyrightability of the work is not judged by the skill or training of the artist. It is not judged by the time it takes to create the work, or by the subject matter. The real-life objects and people of the world depicted in these photographs were not created by me or Mr. Stieglitz. Instead, it is our conception and composition of the scene as reflected in the photograph we created that is protected by copyright. An act of creation can be short in duration, as little time as it takes to hold up a smartphone or lift a Leica single-lens reflex camera to one's eye and focus and click. It is the mind of the artist working that counts—the framing, the composition, the F-stop, the light/dark levels, the exposure, the clarity of the focus— all of these are creative choices that involve a work of the mind that can be reflected in the work of the artist. And copyright protects these works.

Copyrightable works do not have to be great works of art. Over a hundred and fourteen years ago in the 1903 case of *Bleistein v. Donaldson Lithographing Company*,[5] a wise old United States Supreme Court Justice Oliver Wendell Holmes once evaluated a copyright case, and told us,

> It would be a dangerous undertaking for persons trained only to the law to constitute themselves final judges of the worth of pictorial illustrations, outside of the narrowest and most obvious limits. At the one extreme some works of genius would be sure to miss appreciation. Their very novelty would make them repulsive until the public had learned the new language in which their author spoke.[6]

Justice Holmes considered the copyrightability of a commercial advertisement poster produced using a chromolithographic technique:[7]

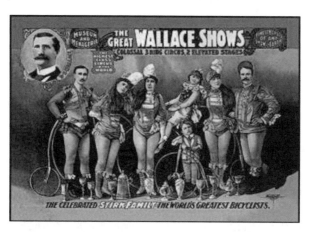

The question of worth mattered because, at the time, copyright was stingy as to its protection of visual art works—only certain, truly expressive works of art would be protected under copyright—and Justice Holmes had to determine if this circus poster was creative and artistic enough to be covered by copyright law. Based on the recommendation made in the quoted portion above, Homes held that the chromolithographic poster was copyrightable. United States law has stayed on this course since 1903—an author can receive a copyright on any expressive creation no matter how crude, humble, or pedestrian it may seem to others. But it has to be original and created by you.

The average traveler's vacation snap shots may never have been confused with art in your own mind or in those with whom you share such snap shots. On occasion, you may have achieved brilliance with your camera or smartphone, but rarely thought to mount a one-person exhibition of your photographs. The point is, copyright doesn't care if you are highly skilled, well known, or truly creative in the layperson's usage of that word. Copyright protects an author from only one thing: unauthorized copying. It does not guaranty talent or imagination or value or anything else about the works that fall within its purview.

As discussed above, the public policy of copyright is to benefit the public first and foremost, not to reward authors for good works. The low bar to copyright protection benefits the general public by encouraging the production of new works. With only four bottom-line requirements for copyright—Original-Expression-Created by the Author-Fixed in a Tangible Medium—no one should be deterred from creating new works and seeking to protect them from copying.

Clip Art Used in Original, Creative Works

Inevitably, authors and artists make use of the creations of others in their own work. Some of this earlier material is public domain (no longer or never protected by copyright), and other material is used fairly (as will be discussed in the Fair Use chapter of this book, Chapter 9). The second artist cannot obtain a new copyright on the portions of earlier works not conceived of and created by the artist, but the second artist can obtain a copyright over new material, including new arrangements that create new content, meaning, and expression different from the old material. A shorthand way of expressing this concept may be demonstrated using clip art.

Clip art, in the common understanding of the term, is not protected by copyright, and so it is public domain material that may be used by a new author or artist. If the second artist makes a creative, original arrangement of the non-original raw material, the second artist could receive a new copyright on the compilation, the new arrangement, and any new expression that emerges from the artist's conception and creation. No one can copy the exact compilation and arrangement, although new artists could take the same raw material and make different arrangements of their own, and receive a new copyright on their new, original arrangements and compilations.

Photocopies as Original, Creative Works

Pushing the concepts even further, consider the "art" of photocopying. A photocopy machine might seem to be the least original and creative art-making device known to man. It exists to copy. But unpacking the issue further, you might recognize that a photocopy machine is a large and clumsy camera with a limited ability (or need) to focus, and usually it has only a few controls for light/dark balance, contrast, and size of image. Yet, it is a camera, and you might put your brain to work conceiving of new ways to use this tool to create new works with new expression just by playing with the few controls the photocopy machine has—contrast, light/dark balance, and size of image—as well as by placing the original image on the glass in a new orientation:[8]

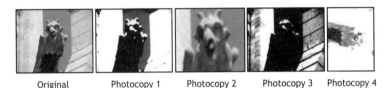

Original   Photocopy 1   Photocopy 2   Photocopy 3   Photocopy 4

You could receive a new copyright for every one of the photocopied images because each is new, original to the author (the operator of the photocopy machine), and each reveals a new conception from the mind of the author that was rendered into a tangible expression in the new images produced. Note that this example assumes you had a right to make copies of all or large portions of the original image; if you didn't have the right to copy by license, permission, public domain status, or fair use, then your efforts to enjoy a new copyright would potentially be thwarted by the enforcement of the original artist's copyright.

New copyrights for new photocopies would not be possible if you just used the machine to make duplicates of the original image one after the other. The law calls this a "slavish" copying endeavor. It is true that a careful observer who is familiar with the performance of photocopy machines might be able to detect the minute variations in each photocopy and note their differences from the original. But this matters not, because you, the purported "author," were not engaging your mind in a creative endeavor. You were trying to copy, not make a new, original work, and that's not going to produce a creative work sufficient to merit copyright protection. Your motive and state of mind matter.

An Endeavor to Copy: *Meshwerks v. Toyota*

The photocopy example is a good lead-in a real case: *Meshwerks v. Toyota*.[9] The circumstances of this lawsuit were that Meshwerks had worked with Toyota to create 3-dimensional images of Toyota cars that would be used in internet applications where shoppers could look at the cars from all sides and change the colors of the car as they compared vehicles. Meshwerks used digital modeling to copy the designs of the Toyota cars. The whole idea was to make very accurate duplicates of the Toyota cars in a 3-D digital form.

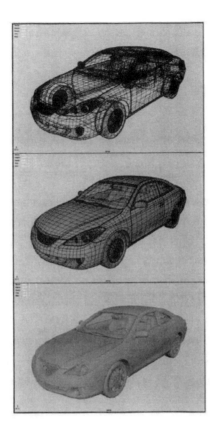

The techniques used were sophisticated and required a lot of time, effort, training, and skill. When the relationship between Meshwerks and Toyota ended, Toyota retained the works and started to use them in other applications. Meshwerks objected—it had not sold or assigned a copyright over the 3-D works to Toyota, nor agreed in the parties' contract as to how the works would be used after the parties went their separate ways. Meshwerks sued Toyota to prevent it from exploiting the works.

Toyota defended by asserting that Meshwerks did not have a copyright over the 3-D works. Yes, the works were skillful and inventive, but they were held to be copies of other works, not produced through a conception of a new, original work that was then executed into a tangible work by Meshwerks. The motive to duplicate, to replicate the pre-existing appearance of the Toyota cars, mattered to the court. The expressions achieved were not original to Meshwerks, and Meshwerks had no copyright over them. The court accepted Toyota's reasoning, and denied Meshwerk's copyright claim.

Digital Copies—Not Original, Not Copyrightable

We can go further than the photocopy technology of the last fifty or sixty years in evaluating the concept of "slavish" copying vs. original creation of works. The modern technology of digital file duplication is a more perfect example of exact duplication than that of a photocopy. If an artist reproduces her digital art by copying the .jpeg, .png, or .gif file without doing anything else to the image, she cannot receive a separate copyright for the copy. A copy of digitalized art is not separately copyrightable—each copy is an exact duplicate of the original to the degree that our minds can hardly conceive of anything that is more exactly a duplicate.

Copyright: No Pain, No Sweat Required

Effort does not matter to copyright. Training does not matter. Sweat and tears do not matter. You can work hard for weeks over a work or take a snap shop in a matter of seconds. All that matters is did you conceive of something new, original to you, and did you then create it. Much of this returns us to the public policy behind copyright, and what it protects and prevents. Copyright serves the public interest by encouraging and protecting the creation of any new work in any media. But all it protects the work from is unauthorized copying. Copyright is a monopoly, but it is a monopoly over the right to duplicate a single work. Copyright does not guaranty commercial success or even suggest financial gain or salability of the protected work. Copyright status does not speak to a work's value or quality.

Setting the (Low) Standard of Creativity and Originality

There are few limits to copyrightable subject matter beyond those we spoke of earlier—ideas, processes, procedures, concepts, methods, and the like. You can copyright obscene and outrageous material such as pornography or obscenity. You can copyright false and fraudulent material. Just be creative and original when you do it.

The standard of creativity and originality in copyright is a very low standard, and this is intentional. As Justice Holmes said, we don't want to leave out cutting edge, avante garde art like Goya or Manet in their times, nor art that appeals to less developed tastes. We don't want to exclude experimental poetry or stream-of-consciousness free verse writing. We don't want to exclude the goofiest YouTube video or amateur musical recording. Professor Melville Nimmer, the author of one of the most famous copyright treatises in the United States, said: "If a work might arguably be regarded as a work of art by any meaningful segment of the population, high brow, low brow, hippy, avante garde . . ."[10] etc., then it qualifies for copyright.

Copyright has no requirement of quality let alone excellence, because all it protects against is copying. No one gets to duplicate your original creative work. It does not tie up any other similar works that predate your work or are otherwise not deemed to be copies of your work.

The standard of originality also is a very low standard. It is little more than a prohibition on actual copying. It does not require uniqueness or one of a kind status. Anything more than a mere trivial variation that is intentionally conceived of and created by the author meets the standard.

Victor Whitmill v. Warner Brothers,[11] and the Copyrightability of Tribal Tattoos

The originality of tribal tattoos presents a new question for our consideration: Did S. Victor Whitmill, the tattoo artist of the tribal-style tattoo on the face of former boxing champion Mike Tyson, produce a work that is copyrightable and protectable? This question mattered a great deal in a recent dispute when Mr. Whitmill's tattoo was quite apparently duplicated on actor Ed Helms' face for the movie, *The Hangover Part II*.[12]

Regarding the bottom-line requirements of copyright—expression, fixed in a tangible medium, original (not copied), conceived of in the mind of the author—there is no dispute that Victor Whitmill rendered this expression into existence in a fixed and tangible medium (noting that "fixed" pertains to perceptibility and not immovability). But the analysis of originality and creativity is more complicated:

Originality—Whitmill may have decided on the design, but it is possible he copied an existing tribal tattoo. (In the actual complaint, Whitmill alleged that it was an original design, not a copy.[13]) If the tattoo design was original to the tattoo artist, then the work is copyrightable. If it is a copy of a pre-existing design, a present or historical tribal mark, or one of a genre of tribal markings that the tattoo artist simply adopted and decided to put to use in a facial tattoo for his customer, Mike Tyson, then the work is non-original.

Creativity—We have every reason to believe that the tattoo artist created the tattoo on Tyson's face, but that is only half of the analysis. If he didn't conceive of the design as something original to him, then he won't get a copyright for copying a pre-existing design.

Telephone Directories as Original, Creative Works

Telephone directories deserve a spot on the list of examples of how the originality and creativity requirements of copyright work because the issue was litigated at great length in the United States, in a case that went all the way to the United States Supreme Court: *Feist Publications v. Rural Telephone Service Company.*[14] The facts of the case are relatively simple: the defendant was accused of copying plaintiff's telephone directory. But the case turned on whether the plaintiff's telephone directory was original and creative and therefore copyrightable in the first place. It turned out not to be, and thus the plaintiff had no copyright to enforce in the litigation.

You will follow this line of thinking easily now that you have considered all of the examples above on how the law works: the author didn't create the names and telephone numbers that appeared in the book; the names and numbers were preexisting, not conceived of and rendered into existence by the author. The author might have conceived of a brand new arrangement for the names and numbers, much as was done in the example using the turkey clip art, but here the author employed a well-used, tried and true, preexisting arrangement: the names and their numbers were listed in alphabetical order. That order and arrangement was not original to this author, it was copied or borrowed.

A creative, original arrangement of telephone data was recognized as copyrightable in a case involving a Chinatown telephone directory, *Key Publications, Inc. v. Chinatown Today Pub. Enterprises.*[15] The plaintiffs had made a new (original) selection and arrangement of telephone numbers focusing only on businesses that spoke Chinese. Because the selection and arrangement was new, not copied, and it was conceived of and created by the author, and it had new expression (new meaning and message from the selection and compilation), then it met the copyright requirements. Note that only the new parts, the new selection and arrangement, were copyrightable. The preexisting names and telephone numbers of the businesses were not a part of the plaintiff's copyright. Other persons could come along, take the same data as to the names and numbers of these businesses, and make their own selection, compilation, and arrangement of the data. But these persons will not be able to copy plaintiff's particular selection, compilation, and arrangement.

Creativity and the "Fixed in a Tangible Medium" Requirement

Normally the "fixed in a tangible medium" requirement is not an issue in the copyright world. An author or artist creates tangible, solid works with a high degree of permanence—books, articles, paintings, sculptures, and prints—and wants people to see and appreciate the work. But in some expressive endeavors, fixation in the act of creation requires a bit more thought.

Speeches, lectures, stage directions, or choreography directions that are not written down or recorded

> Oral expressions may be unique and creative and original to the author, but they are not fixed. The law provides that if a simultaneous recording is made, then the oral expressions and the recording become protected by copyright. Choreography may be fixed in verbal, pictorial, audio, or audio-visual form with notes, drawings, photographs, or a video recording.

An actual performance of a play or other live event or reenactment

> An actual performance of a play or other live event or reenactment is not copyrightable unless it is filmed or recorded or otherwise fixed in media.

Improvised music or other improvised performance

> If you are following the trend here, you will anticipate than a performance of improvised music is not copyrightable unless it is recorded or notated. Music typically receives several copyrights: a copyright for the musical composition (the score, the notation, the sheet music), a separate copyright for the lyrics (as poetry and literature), and a separate copyright for any audio or audiovisual recordings of the work. Improvised music is spontaneous, and supposedly unpredictable; the musician does not necessarily know where she is going with the music or where it will wind up. Most improv artists would resist the notion of planning and notating a performance; it simply is anathema to the genre. Nonetheless, a master of improvised music should get in the habit of writing a sketch of musical notations and verbal descriptions of what she created after it is performed in the improvised session, or at the very least, she should make a

simultaneous recording of the performance even if it is just to fix the work in a tangible media. If the musician does not simultaneously record it, then anyone in the crowd who makes a recording will have created a fixed and tangible expression of the performance that would afford the taper in the crowd an opportunity to copy the performance and even receive a copyright for the selection the taper captured and created in the form of her recording.

Copyrightability of an Installation of Wildflowers

There are instances when courts will demand more permanence and fixed-ness than an artist is able to deliver. The *Kelley v. Chicago Park District*[16] is one such case. *Kelley* tells the tale of Chapman Kelley, an artist of landscapes (as opposed to a landscaper or floral designer) who created a large pictorial display of living wildflowers in Grant Park in downtown Chicago, titled *Wildflower Works*.[17] Later, Chicago wanted to cut the whole thing down in size, changing and replanting the contents of the work. Kelley sought to stop them.

Kelley's Plan for Wildflower Works
http://www.artsjournal.com/aestheticgrounds/KelleyChicagoAerial.JPG

Wildflower Works Installation
http://clancco.com/wp/wp-content/uploads/2011/02/CWFW1992.jpg

Kelley's primary claim was under a section of the copyright code called the Visual Artists Rights Act, which might prevent the reshaping and reduction of the work *if* it were a copyrightable work to begin with, meaning original, creative, expressive, fixed in a tangible medium. The Seventh Circuit federal court of appeals found that the *Wildflowers Works* installation was original and expressive, but that it could not be copyrightable because of the nature of the living media, wildflowers, which were held to be not fixed in a tangible media, and it was not created (as in authored) by Kelley.[18]

The Seventh Circuit denied Kelley his claim to authorship of the work, but its logic is not without its flaws.[19] Regarding authorship, apparently the court thought the author of *Wildflower Works* was God or Mother Nature, never mind that it was Kelley who designed, arranged, compiled, and created the installation. The work is made up of plants, and Kelley didn't create the plants (God did), so he is not the author of the plants. The plants make up the garden; Kelley is responsible for the garden being there, but he did not create the plants in the garden, so see the first answer here.

On fixation, the Seventh Circuit noted that plants sway in the breeze, they move, they grow, they wither, they die. Therefore, they are not fixed. The Seventh Circuit's analysis is short-sighted in several respects. Fixation is not dependent on media. To assure that copyright law remained media neutral, Congress defined fixation of works to include "any tangible medium of expression, now known or later developed, from which they can be perceived, reproduced, or otherwise communicated, either directly or with the aid of a machine or device."[20] Congress further defined "fixed" to mean:

> A work is "fixed" in a tangible medium of expression when its embodiment in a copy . . . is sufficiently permanent or stable to permit it to be perceived, reproduced, or otherwise communicated for a period of more than transitory duration. A work consisting of sounds, images, or both, that are being transmitted, is "fixed" for purposes of this title if a fixation of the work is being made simultaneously with its transmission[.][21]

Contrary to the Seventh Circuit's highly restrictive notion of fixation, fixation is supposed to be a simple, open-ended, painfully easy to satisfy concept. The ability to perceive the creation is all that matters, and you can even use machines to do the perception. If the creation is oral or fleeting or otherwise transitory in nature, you can record it with a longer-lasting media such as a visual, audio, or audio-visual recording that depicts or records the creation.

Wildflower Works met each of the fixation criteria. It could be seen, felt, smelt, and tasted if you wanted to. It existed in drawings, photographs, and other depictions and descriptions. Its nature was known well enough to copy it or avoid copying it. The nature of the creation was no mystery to anyone.

The criticism that a work cannot be a painting because it consists of living items mistakes media for creation of expression. Every painting is made of something—its media. At some level of immediacy, the media is traceable to a natural organic or chemical substance that was formed or grown in or on the earth. The canvas is traced to cotton duck or linen, which is traced to the cotton plant, which grew out of the earth. The stretcher bars are made of wood which grew up as a tree. The paint medium might be a naturally occurring substance such as charcoal or raw umber, or a slightly more complicated composition of lapis lazuli and linseed oil making ultramarine, or a chemical composition of matter constituting Prussian blue or one of the many synthetic hues that have become the normal media in artistic production. Sculpted media is similarly situated, substituting only a natural or manipulated media of clay, stone, metal, or a casting media that is plastic (i.e., malleable, able to be molded or shaped).

The fact that creations of living media might move, or change, or grow, or wither and die and decompose again is not probative of copyright creativity. Consider that any work using wildflowers or some other living, organic media could be frozen in time by encasing it in Lucite or actually keeping it frozen at a sufficiently low temperature to keep it from decaying. Does that make the expression of the work different—regarding as we must that it is the expression of the work that causes us to think of copyright protection at all. Even absent that treatment, the comparison of the mobility of one form of work vs. another simply is a matter of degree: all painting surfaces are susceptible to expansion and contraction from humidity levels and temperature; they just move at so small a rate that we would hardly trouble to measure it. Sculptures of stone may be less moveable from temperature than metal, but again, the movement in each case is hardly noticeable. The movement by wind and air current works a great effect on wildflowers and plants in the great outdoors, less so indoors, but not much less than the workings of air currents on paper mobiles and other delicate sculptures. All materials degrade over time, although with some care there are media that seem "permanent." All that this reflects is our comfort level with a semblance of permanence corresponding to our time of observation in the presence of the work. A highly fugitive dye placed in direct sunlight will give up its color faster than a wildflower. Neither is permanent, yet the chemical media will not draw the attention of a jurist in the manner that living media will.

Last, the fact that some artistic installations might resemble something else—a garden—is not a question concerning copyrightability, it is one of aesthetics and philosophy. If the issue was, is this art, we might ponder for a time whether an expressive composition of living matter was sufficiently artistic to meet our standards when it was created by a self-proclaimed gardener as opposed to a self-proclaimed or externally certified artist. We tend not to credit the work of first-time amateurs as high art, although on occasion the results are very intricate and beautiful. Nevertheless, the issue here is copyrightability, and the artistic merit of the work or the creator never has been a requirement for copyrightability.

And what makes living media expressive? Color, shape, forms, textures—all of which are possessed by wildflowers and living media as well and often to a greater degree than other media, such as paint in tubes, blank canvas, or a mound of sculpting clay. The same attributes of color, shape, forms, and textures that provide the difference in the expression perceived from a blank white canvas compared to that of a highly detailed landscape are provided by a palate of wildflowers combined and arranged on dark earth.

Kelley is a peculiar case, not necessarily predictive of future cases; but for now, it exists as a precedent in the law.

[1]   Michael D. Murray, Cropped and resized photograph of the Michael D. Murray painting, *Brookings Hall, Washington University in St. Louis* (2016).

[2]   *Burrow-Giles Lithographic Co. v. Sarony*, 111 U.S. 53 (1884).

[3]   Michael D. Murray, Cropped and resized photographs (clockwise from top left) of a 1974 Cadillac Eldorado Convertible (2013); Palm Trees at the JW Marriott Resort in Palm Desert, CA (2012); and the author and his wife in front of a recreation of the Temple of Heaven at the Missouri Botanical Gardens in St. Louis, MO (2012).

[4]   Michael D. Murray, Cropped and resized images of public domain photographs by Alfred Stieglitz (clockwise from top left): *The Terminal* (1893); *Night Reflections* (1896); and *West Street* (1893).

[5]   *Bleistein v. Donaldson Lithographing Co.*, 188 U.S. 239 (1903).

[6]   *Id.* at 251.

[7]   Michael D. Murray, Cropped and resized image of a chromolithographic advertisement poster for the Great Wallace Shows c. 1903, the subject of *Bleistein v. Donaldson Lithographing Co.*, 188 U.S. 239 (1903).

[8]   Images: Michael D. Murray, Thumbnail-Sized Reproductions of Original and Four Photocopy Manipulations of Michael D. Murray's Photograph of a Gargoyle at Sacré-Cœur Basilica in Paris (2014).

[9]   *Meshwerks, Inc. v. Toyota Motor Sales USA, Inc.*, 528 F.3d 1258 (10th Cir. 2008).

[10]   1 MELVILLE B. NIMMER & DAVID NIMMER, NIMMER ON COPYRIGHT § 2.08[B][1] (2006).

[11]   This example is based on the lawsuit between Victor Whitmill and Warner Brothers for the use without permission of Whitmill's copyrighted tattoo featured on the face of the boxer Mike Tyson, an alleged reproduction of which was later used on actor Ed Helms' face in The Hangover Part II. *See* Meredith Hatic, *Who Owns Your Body Art?: The Copyright and Constitutional Implications of Tattoos*, 23 FORDHAM INTELL. PROP. MEDIA & ENT. L.J. 396, 398 (2012); Yolanda M. King, *The Enforcement Challenges for Tattoo Copyrights*, 2014 J. INTELL. PROP. L. 22, 29. This lawsuit ultimately settled. Matthew Belloni, *"Hangover" Tattoo Lawsuit Settled*, REUTERS (June 20, 2011, 10:48 PM), http://www.reuters.com/article/2011/06/21/us-hangover-idUSTRE75K0DF20110621.

[12]   Images here: Michael D. Murray, Thumbnail-Sized Excerpts of Exhibits from the Verified Complaint for Injunctive Relief and Damages, *S. Victor Whitmill v. Warner Brothers Entertainment*, No. 4:11-CV-752 (E.D. Mo. April 25, 2011), available at https://www.wired.com/images_blogs/threatlevel/2011/05/tysontattoo.pdf.

[13]   Verified Complaint for Injunctive Relief and Damages, *Whitmill v. Warner Brothers Ent.*, No. 4:11-CV-752, at para.1.

[14]   *Feist Publications, Inc. v. Rural Tel. Serv. Co.*, 499 U.S. 340 (1991).

[15]   *Key Publications, Inc. v. Chinatown Today Pub. Enterprises, Inc.*, 945 F.2d 509, 512-13 (2d Cir. 1991).

[16]   *Kelley v. Chicago Park Dist.*, 635 F.3d 290 (7th Cir. 2011).

[17]   Images: Michael D. Murray, Thumbnail-Sized Excerpt of Kelley's Plan for Wildflower Works (2015); Michael D. Murray, Thumbnail-Sized Excerpt of Wildflower Works Installation (2015), both the subject of *Kelley v. Chicago Park Dist.*, 635 F.3d 290 (7th Cir. 2011).

[18]   *Kelley*, 635 F.3d at 303 ("The real impediment to copyright here is not that Wildflower Works fails the test for originality (understood as 'not copied' and 'possessing some creativity') but that a living garden lacks the kind of authorship and stable fixation normally required to support copyright. . . .").

[19]   This section's discussion regarding the intersecting requirements of creativity and fixation in general, and the critique of the Seventh Circuit's opinion in Kelley in particular, draws heavily from Michael D. Murray, *Post-Myriad Genetics Copyright of Synthetic Biology and Living Media*, 10 OKLA. J. L. & TECH. 71, 106-08 (2014).

[20]   17 U.S.C. § 102(a).

[21]   17 U.S.C. § 101 (definition of "fixed").

CHAPTER 3

Ideas vs. Expressions

The lessons of originality and creativity lead directly to the next major topic of copyright law, ideas vs. expressions: **Ideas** are not protected by copyright. **Expressions** of ideas are. This simple statement leads to one of the most troublesome areas of copyright law: the **idea-expression distinction.** Authors, artists, lawyers, and judges must learn to differentiate the idea from the expression of the idea in a work, because one who copies the former is a valued contributor to the arts or literature, but one who copies the latter is a potential infringer of another person's copyrighted work. The huge problem with this scenario is that we cannot encounter ideas outside of our own head separate from their embodiment in a communicative media, such as speech, writing, visual imagery, audio, or audio-visual recording. Somehow, an author or artist who wants to express an idea encountered in other persons' works must discern the common "idea" and express or depict the idea without infringing the other works' expression. This chapter will illustrate the law's approach to this process.

The Idea of a Scene and Expressions of That Idea

There have been many depictions of the "Birth of Venus"[1] over the years:

| Botticelli | Boucher | Bouguereau |

| Poussin | Cabanel |

This fact illustrates the topic of this chapter: anyone can follow up on the idea of a goddess born from the ocean, arriving beautiful, glorious, and nude, attended by mythical beings or other gods. But no one can copy the depiction of the birth of Venus-Aphrodite already created by another artist unless that earlier work is in the public domain or otherwise is no longer subject to copyright protection.

Genres, Schools, Movements, and Trends

The Idea-Expression Distinction allows the creation and development of genres of literature, schools or movements of art, and trends in media and entertainment of all kinds. Works of a certain genre of literature follow certain ideas about setting, characters, perspective, plot, the unraveling of the plot, and the typical climax or denouement. Edgar Allen Poe and Wilkie Collins created a genre of writing—the mystery-detective-crime story—but anyone is able to follow in their footsteps and use the ideas, themes, and devices they pioneered to make their work feel and sound like a proper mystery crime novel with a detective protagonist.

The idea expression distinction allows certain characters (wizards) and settings (a world where magic is real), and certain storylines and story arcs (a hero's journey, overcoming obstacles, until finding success or redemption at the end) to be repeated in innumerable works. Many stories can use these formulas, and no one need start to question whether the *Harry Potter* seven-book series copied the *Lord of the Rings* trilogy. But while there can be dozens of stories about children with magical powers, and even a few that attend the same school together, all of these stories better not take place at a magical school of witchcraft and wizardry that features broomstick sports, magic classes on potions, divination, and defense against the dark arts, and a teenage hero with a remarkable resistance to a certain powerful dark lord, because these particular aspects of the story taken together are J.K. Rowlings' particular expression of several tried-and-true magic and fantasy story formulas.

Schools and movements in art follow certain ideas and principles important to the school or movement. For example, in the visual art of painting, a change to *plein air* (in the open air) from studio painting, and from the depiction of historical, mythical, and religious subjects to everyday scenes and subjects, defined ideas that were important to the Impressionist movement. The abstraction and rejection of figures, shapes, and proportion were important to several "modern" and contemporary movements in art, and the use of ubiquitous images (cartoons, famous products' trade dress, and commercial advertising themes) defined what would be called Pop Art. All of these exemplify the possibility to copy and use an idea about art without necessarily duplicating other persons' art works.

Trends in entertainment are, well, trendy, growing and waning, coming and going. An idea, such as realty TV programming may be copied and followed *ad nauseum*, and I mean that quite literally. Anyone can take their shot at taking a reality-based television concept and embodying and expressing their own take on it—the emphasis being on "their own" take, not a taking of another person's embodiment and expression of the concept. So-called "copycat" programming is allowed to copy the ideas, themes, and general concepts of a trend of programming, but they cannot copy one specific author's embodiment and expression of the idea. There can be a dozen reality-genre, human-competition, team-based programs running all at the same time, but no one can copy the particular show called *Survivor* in all of its particulars.

Many paintings of a certain school or movement of art will resemble each other, as seen in the Impressionist paintings by Monet and Renoir, or the cubist paintings of Braque and Picasso shown below, but each can follow or embody an idea without copying the work of another artist.

| Claude Monet, *Bain à la Grenouillère* (1869) | Pierre-Auguste Renoir, *La Grenouillère* (1869) |

Claude Monet, *Bain à la Grenouillère II* (1869)

Pierre-Auguste Renoir, *La Grenouillère III* (1869)

Pablo Picasso, *Portrait of Daniel-Henry Kahnweiler* (1910)

Georges Braque, *Le Portugais-The Emigrant* (1911-12)

Pablo Picasso, *Les Damoseil D' Avignon* (1907)

Georges Braque, *Large Nude* (1908)

If the resemblance between two works comes from the use of certain themes, formulas, or artistic techniques used in a genre, school, or movement of art, chances are the two works can happily coexist. As discussed above, for copyright to get involved, there must be copying, and random independent creation that uses common themes, formulas, or artistic techniques of a genre, school, or movement of art is not copying.

If two works are similar, the idea-expression step of the analysis is to determine why they are similar, and decide whether they are similar for copying a particular idea (concept, theme, dramatic device, story arch, etc.), or are they similar because specific parts of the first work are actually copied and reproduced in the second work; not just the ideas behind the first work, but the expressions and embodiments of these ideas that are particular to the first work.

Inventive, Innovative Ideas

The author who communicates truly inventive, innovative, and clever ideas surely deserves protection from copying in our intellectual property legal scheme. The question is, does copyright provide that protection, and the answer is "No." Patent law can provide intellectual property protection for truly inventive ideas, but it has strict requirements for true inventions that were not obvious to persons skilled in the prior art,[2] and only locks the information up for twenty years.[3] But the concepts of "creative" and "creativity" in copyright law do not mean inventive or novel. And copyright's term lasts a whole lot longer than patent law's term—the lifetime of the author plus 70 years. That is one reason why no idea, no process, no procedure, no formula or recipe with practical application, can be tied up under copyright protection. An idea, no matter how inventive, novel, and artistically innovative, is not copyrightable and cannot be protected through copyright law.

Independent Creation of Works That Embody the Same Idea

The concepts of an idea vs. an expression of an idea are not always easy to distinguish, but some scenarios are easier to predict than others.[4] Consider the following:

Scenario 1: Two authors meet for drinks. Author One says to Author Two, "We need more realistic, gritty, television competition shows. We should film unrehearsed, live competitions where people battle it out in teams. Maybe in some place people don't get to very often." Both authors agree that this sounds like a good idea.

The two authors part ways. Author One goes home and creates the television show, *Survivor*, where a group of competitors are divided into tribes and live in difficult conditions on a remote island while they battle each other to win favors, called talismans and immunities, until one by one the team members are eliminated, all of which is filmed unrehearsed, in the raw, then later cut and edited for viewing. Author Two goes home and creates, *America's Top Chef*, where a group of competitors are divided into chef teams and live and work together in dorms, and perform difficult culinary tasks in a battle to win favors, privileges, and protections, until one by one the team members are eliminated, all of which is filmed unrehearsed, in the raw, then later cut and edited for viewing. Is there a copyright problem here yet?

Not yet. First of all, nothing from the meeting of the two authors was written down, nothing was in a tangible medium. The two were only talking. Second, you cannot copyright a theme—the idea—for a game show. That is an idea, and as such, it is not copyrightable. Third, even if there was more to the scenario, the two shows do not sound very similar. So, no copyright issue yet.

Scenario 2: Author Three is watching television and sees an episode of *Survivor*. She is inspired, and runs out and creates *Big Brother*, where a group of competitors are divided into two teams who have to share a house and perform some embarrassing tasks until one by one the team members are eliminated, all of which is filmed by hidden cameras, unrehearsed, in the raw, then later cut and edited for viewing. Copyright problem?

Probably not. Once Author One has taken the raw idea for a show and put it into a detailed expression, for instance, the show *Survivor*, there will be elements of her expression of the idea that she will be able to protect with copyright law. But the two shows must be at least similar, and so far, the only similarities are things that do not sound very creative and original to Author One. There have been competitions with teams from time immemorial. There have been other unrehearsed television shows filmed in the raw, then later cut and edited for viewing. There have been many shows where contestants are eliminated until a champion remains. Living in a house together does not sound much like living on a remote island together. So, Author Three need not go out and hire a lawyer, yet.

Scenario 3: Author One and Author Two meet again for drinks. Author One is all excited about her *Survivor* project. She has brought sketches of the island set, written descriptions of the rules to gain "talismans" and "immunities," and she is especially excited to show Author Two several drawings of Tiki-style gods that will symbolize each tribe in the competition. She wants to know what Author Two thinks. Author Two is circumspect, says a few nice things about the project, but leaves shortly thereafter for "an engagement." Then Author Two goes right to work creating a television show called *Tiki Challenge*, which uses an island set that looks a lot like *Survivor*'s, it has the same rules to get "protections" and "immunities," it uses the term "tribes" for the teams, and it uses large Tiki-style gods to symbolize the tribes in the competition.

Scenario 3 presents a genuine copyright infringement issue. Author One has gone far beyond the idea stage to express the ideas of the show *Survivor* in fixed and tangible expressions that are original to and created by Author One. Author Two obviously had access to the expressions regarding the show—Author One showed them to him. Author Two has copied a large number of the expressions of the aspects of the show—visuals, written rules, terminology—much of which is the creative, original work product of Author One. (We can tell that much of it is creative, original work product, because there is nothing inherent about human competitions that they have to take place on islands, with teams called tribes, under the watch of Tiki gods, to win talismans and immunities). Author Two most likely has infringed Author One's copyright.

Facts About History

You cannot copyright the facts from a realistic account of historical events because the information is facts. Facts are uncopyrightable because they are not created and not original. They are discovered or communicated, but not "authored." There is no copyright for facts or events or even research (meaning the raw data, the things you discover). The author can copyright the expression of the facts in the account. The expression is the exact wording chosen by the author to express the facts. This wording is protected, although the protection most likely will be limited to the exact wording of the author because of the merger doctrine (discussed in Chapter 4).

The Copyright of Non-Fiction Works

Non-fiction works are copyrighted, so you might be wondering what inside these works actually is copyrightable. You now know that facts and data are not copyrightable. If non-fiction works were just a running list of facts, little or nothing in the works would be copyrightable. But the authors express the facts in writing and in charts, diagrams, and illustrations, all of which can be original and creative arrangements of facts and data, and as such, can be copyrighted.

As one example, many authors have written about the life and times and untimely death of President Abraham Lincoln. Much of these accounts may be factual information—especially those writings that are contemporaneous accounts of the times. Anyone can research and collect the factual information from these and other historical sources. But note the words, *factual information*. What you cannot do is simply transcribe (or scan, or copy word-for-word) the write up of history in works that still are under copyright, because the written works are the creative, original *expressions* and arrangement of the uncopyrightable facts and data, and this expression and arrangement is subject to copyright.

There remains a question concerning an authors' inferences, insights, and historical conjectures about the historical events or historical persons they are writing about. For example, the historian, Doris Kearns Goodwin, wrote an account of the Lincoln presidency entitled, *Team of Rivals: The Political Genius of Abraham Lincoln*, which reflects her research into the facts of the presidency, but almost assuredly contains her insights and conjectures into the meaning of and probable ways the events unfolded.

Authors of historical accounts often construct meetings that may not have occurred in history, they make composites of characters or events to cover gaps in the record, and sometimes even invent conversations between historical figures. All of this is done so as to unfold the history in a narrative format (a story), which is a much more interesting, understandable, and readable format than a list of facts and dates. (Newspapers follow the same narrative formula, they publish stories about the news of the day, not just a list of facts; that is why we call newspaper stories "the first draft of history.")

This brings us back to Doris Kearns Goodwin and her work on Lincoln's presidency. If a movie-maker reads Goodwin's work, and is inspired by it to make a movie, *The Lincoln Presidency*, and assuming the movie-maker does not intend to obtain a license to use the Goodwin work, there are certain things the movie-maker could use from Goodwin's text, and certain things she could not. Certainly the movie-maker could use the facts, but if one is not a historian, how does one know what are the facts and what are the "something else"? And the "something else" can be divided into standard interpretations and inferences regarding history, widely recognized and accepted, and not particularly attributed to a single author whose work still is under copyright protection. These standard interpretations mostly likely could be copied, although again, it would be hard for non-historians to know exactly what these are. Lastly, are the unique, original, creative inferences and conjectures of Goodwin herself. These are protected by Goodwin's copyright. Again, could you tell this material from the rest? You could hire a historical consultant, or buy the rights to use Goodwin's book, or do a lot of research into the other historical accounts so that you could know the accepted history from the original contributions of one author. None of these paths is easy, but they are necessary because you are not permitted simply to copy historical non-fiction works.

———

The complexity of the idea-expression distinction along with the basic requirements of originality and creativity have led to several doctrines of copyright law that drill down even further into the analysis of what kinds of content are copyrightable: the scènes à faire and merger doctrines, and the utilitarian and functional works doctrine. These doctrines are the subjects of the next two chapters.

---

[1]   Michael D. Murray, Collage of Thumbnail Excerpts of Five Public Domain Paintings of the Birth of Venus by Sandro Botticelli (c.1486), François Boucher (1740), William-Adolphe Bouguereau (1879), Nicolas Poussin (1635), and Alexandre Cabanel (1863).

[2]   35 U.S.C. § 103; *KSR Int'l Co. v. Teleflex Inc.*, 550 U.S. 398, 399 (2007); *Graham v. John Deere Co. of Kansas City*, 383 U.S. 1, 12-13 (1966).

[3]   35 U.S.C. § 154(a)(1) and (2); *Kimble v. Marvel Entm't, LLC*, 135 S. Ct. 2401, 2415 (2015).

[4]   The specific scenarios and discussion here are taken from my earlier works, 1 LEONARD DUBOFF, MICHAEL D. MURRAY ET AL., ART LAW DESKBOOK: ARTISTS' RIGHTS IN INTELLECTUAL PROPERTY, MORAL RIGHTS, AND FREEDOM OF EXPRESSION, ch. 1 (2017), and LEONARD DUBOFF & MICHAEL D. MURRAY, ART LAW: CASES AND MATERIALS, ch. 2 (2d ed. 2017).

CHAPTER 4

Scènes à Faire and Merger

As noted above, only an author's particularly original and creative expressions of facts and ideas of the world and things in the world can achieve copyright protection. This limitation extends to the expression or "depiction" of abstract concepts such as truth, faith, fidelity, and wisdom, and to the expression or depiction of more concrete facts, such as the common appearance or attributes of a natural subject. In the literary arts, no one can obtain a copyright monopoly on the words necessary to communicate an idea or concept. In the visual arts, no one can obtain a copyright monopoly on the depiction of the actual appearance of Oscar Wilde, or a realistic depiction of a tiger that features the animal with orangish fur and black slashing stripes because these are characteristics common to all tigers and necessary to include in the work so that the work can communicate the concept of a "tiger" to the viewer. In most cases, the words that are associated with certain concepts and that are necessary to communicate ideas about these concepts were not invented and created by the author any more than the actual appearance of Oscar Wilde or a tiger were not invented and created by any visual artist depicting these subjects. However, each author's individual arrangements, embodiments, and expressions of these subjects are potentially copyrightable. It is the job of copyright law to police the margins of these potential copyrights.

The originality and creativity requirements and the idea-expression distinction lead to two doctrines of copyright law called the **scènes à faire** and **merger doctrines**. The doctrines are directly related to each other, and in some copyright situations they overlap to restrict the kinds of subject matter that may become subject to copyright. The breakdown as far as it can be delineated is as follows:

Scènes à Faire

Scènes à faire may be loosely translated from the French as "scenes that must be done."[1] In the literary arts, the term refers to stock scenes (finding a clue in an unexpected place; fighting over a weapon), stock characters (Irish cops; hard-boiled detectives; femme fatales), genre-required, or story arc-required scenes and sequences of the story or plot (chase scenes; boy meets girl, boy loses girl, boy gets girl back plot lines; foggy nights and rainy London streets; the "big reveal" of a mystery). In the visual arts, scènes à faire includes stock images (a building with a bell over the front door to mean a school; a building with a tower and cross over the front door to mean a church), standard depictions (a hammock, pitcher of lemonade, and sunglasses to mean summertime; a car with suitcases strapped to the roof to mean "on vacation"), the appearance of actual objects (how tigers must be depicted in order to communicate "tiger"), and common themes and ideas associated with life that are not copyrightable and may be appropriated by any artist who wishes to express or depict the scene or the theme. The more realistic the description or depiction of a natural object or scene, the less of the work that can be protected under copyright.

Merger

The **merger doctrine** in copyright law parallels scènes à faire. Merger holds that if there are a limited number of ways to express a concept or idea, then copyright will not afford one author with a monopoly over those limited ways. Copyright law states that in these circumstances the idea and the expression have merged, so that neither one will fall within one author's copyright, and both the idea and the expression will be free to all to use and exploit. Merger is easier to track in literary contexts because there are just so many ways to express a concept in a given language, but it is also used for visual expressions of ideas in situations where a certain depiction is deemed to be both necessary and inevitable, as in taking a photograph of a bottle of Skyy Vodka that must depict the actual bottle of Skyy Vodka.[2]

The Overlap of Scènes à Faire and Merger

Scènes à faire and merger both reflect the fact that much art and literature builds on earlier works, and over time, certain themes, scenes, and ways of describing or depicting things have become standard. Suspenseful stories start on dark and stormy nights; urban police dramas will have an old Irish cop or two on board; Westerns will involve a crime, a hunt down, a confrontation, and a resolution by violence. No one gains any credit or copyright protection from adopting these motifs, passages, or scenes—they simply must be done, as the term states—and they certainly are not created by or original to the artist.

Copyright will exclude from an author's or artist's copyright the portion of the work that is deemed to be scènes à faire or which is subject to the merger doctrine and is therefore "merged" with the idea or concept of the scene. If these doctrines did not exist, much creative, original expression would be foreclosed directly because it contained stock scenes, stock character-types, or standard depictions, and an even broader swath of expression would be foreclosed because it would be viewed as a derivative work of an existing work, and the original copyright holder owns the right to create or authorize works that are derivative of or abstracted from her original work (see Chapter 7 on "Derivative Works").

Merger and Scènes à Faire in Literature

There are a lot of simple examples of the merger doctrine working in literature. With the limitations of language, there are often a limited number of ways of stating certain ideas and concepts. If you want to talk about a dark and stormy night, you are going to have to use words such as dark, stormy, and night, so no author who wrote an earlier description of a dark and stormy night can sue to preclude you from writing your description.

Merger is sometimes described in the context of depicting scenes of a city that show its one greatest landmark—the Eiffel Tower for Paris, the Leaning Tower for Pisa, the Gateway Arch for St. Louis— or common visual elements that are needed to tell the location, or timing, or season, or time period—for example, double-decker buses to indicate London; a shot of the moon and stars to show nighttime; orange leaves on trees to show autumn; clean-shaven soldiers wearing doughboy helmets and leggings and carrying rifles with bayonets to show World War I, as opposed to unshaven soldiers wearing rumpled jungle fatigues with helmets wrapped in mesh nets that hold packs of cigarettes and other small objects and carrying M-16 automatic rifles to indicate the Vietnam War. The idea of nightfall is merged with images that communicate dusk—dim lighting, fading sunset, silhouettes of trees, fireflies appearing, and the like. All of these are uncopyrightable imagery free to be borrowed and exploited by all. In this manner, merger supplements scènes à faire with its "scenes that must be done" concept.

An artist who produces a work that has many uncopyrightable elements—either because the work is non-fictional and contains many facts, or scientific and contains processes or procedures, or because the artist incorporated scènes à faire or merged elements that cannot be monopolized under copyright—is said to hold a "thin copyright" on the work. Thin doesn't mean non-existent; however, it does mean that an alleged infringer will have to have taken a good chunk of the work in order to have copied enough *copyrightable* elements to lead to an actionable case of infringement.

Merger and Scènes à Faire in the Visual Arts

Merger should have less impact in the visual arts because jurists and lawyers should recognize that there are thousands of ways of depicting concepts and themes visually. But merger does play a role in the visual arts when a certain media and artistic technique produces similar outward appearance in works. For example, certain glass blowing techniques will produce milky coloration, others will produce spirals and swirls. These techniques are generally not original to a single artist, and in any event, techniques and procedures are not copyrightable. If a similarity in appearance is attributed to the artists both using the same technique, it should not raise an issue of copyright infringement. And, in other cases, merger is treated as a somewhat stricter version of scènes à faire that requires a finding that the scene and its expression are one in the same. What "one in the same" means in a visual media context is a hard one for me, an artist, to get my head around, but there it is.

A fairly recent litigation between two glass artists illustrates the overlapping coverage of the merger and scènes à faire doctrines: *Satava v. Lowry.*[3] The case discusses the realistic artistic depiction of jellyfishes in sculpted glass media. In the narrative of the case, Lowry (glass artist 2), had been making flat, disc-like jellyfish sculptures, but no one was buying them. One day Lowry strolled into a gallery and saw Satava's (glass artist 1's) works—upright, glass-inside-glass sculptures of realistic-looking jellyfish, looking all the while as if a jellyfish was floating inside a glass sculpture (see illustrations below). Satava's works were selling well. Shortly thereafter, Lowry started making his own upright, glass-inside-glass sculptures of realistic-looking jellyfish. Satava did not appreciate the highest form of flattery and sued to stop Lowry.

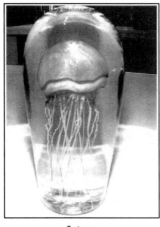 

Satava   Lowry

It is not easy to predict who should prevail in the case just by looking at the two works side-by-side, because although they have similar subject matter (jellyfish), and they both involve one glass sculpture (the jellyfish) inside another (the rounded bullet-shaped "shroud"), they otherwise do not look all that much like each other. But one thing is clear about the case: the merger and scènes à faire doctrines played a role in limiting the scope of Satava's copyright.

One widely accepted method to resolve a problem such as that posed by Satava's original work and Lowry's work emulating Satava's is the **abstraction-filtration-comparison** method; this was the method applied by the court in *Satava v. Lowry*. The abstraction-filtration-comparison method first "abstracts" the constituent elements of the first work, or in more common terms, it dissects the elements of the first work into its separate expressive elements. Then the method strips away ("filters" out) all of the unprotected, uncopyrightable elements that are not original to or created by the first artist, Satava. Afterwards, the stripped down work is compared to the competing work to determine if the competing work still copies any of the copyrightable elements that remain in the first work.

Here, Satava is using a pre-existing glass sculpting technique, glass-in-glass, so the rounded, bullet-shape of the outer glass that is associated with the technique is not original to or created by Satava, and is not part of his copyright. Satava is doing very realistic work with jellyfish, but he cannot claim the actual appearance of jellyfish as part of his copyright (scènes à faire and merger preclude this), so most of the jellyfishy elements of his work are not deemed to be original to or created by him. The court thought it very likely that most artists would depict a jellyfish floating upright, as shown in both works above, so this orientation was not credited to Satava as an original, creative element. After the method stripped down Satava's copyright, all that was left was the exact number, shape, and color of the tentacles of the jellyfish, which Lowry appears *not* to have copied. Lowry prevailed in the litigation.

Comparison of Photographs for Their "Total Concept, Look, and Feel"

The alternative to the abstraction—filtration—comparison method is to compare the **total concept, look, and feel** of the two works for substantial similarity, and then examine whether the similarity is between elements that are arranged in a creative, original manner. For a fairly straightforward application of that test, I return to a case "at bar," namely the Skyy Vodka case I referenced earlier, *Ets-Hokin v. Skyy Vodka.*[4]

In this comparison of photographs of Skyy Vodka bottles, the two photographs are similar—substantially similar, in fact—but the reason for that conclusion is fairly obvious: it is because the two photographs show the same object, a Skyy Vodka bottle. If that is the only important feature of similarity, we don't have much of a copyright case to talk about. In fact, that is the ultimate conclusion of the case.

As discussed in Chapter 2, photographs normally are copyrightable because the photographer brings creative elements to the scene: framing, composition, exposure, and more. But in *Ets-Hokin*, the first photographer took a straight shot, head on, upright picture of a Skyy vodka bottle, so the "total concept, look, and feel" of the elements of interest in the picture originate with the Skyy bottle in its normal, upright orientation, and do not originate with the first photographer. Anyone else photographing a Skyy bottle in a typical straight, head on angle, in an upright orientation, would produce a picture that replicated a great deal of the total concept, look, and feel of the appearance of the Skyy bottle in the first photograph unless the second photographer went to great pains to avoid creating this image.

Here's another set of images, from the case, *Mannion v. Coors:*[5]

Photographer One (Mannion, who photographed basketball star, Kevin Garnett) thought that Photographer Two (of the Coors ad) copied the first image, but cropped it, reversed the image to create a mirror-image, and took it from color to grayscale. This may sound like a lot of changes, but the number of changes is not the issue, and the changes have to be original, and not some feature on Photoshop. Instead, what pops out at you in both photos is the jewelry worn by Garnett, and his enormous, heavily veined hands. Leaving aside the mirror-image and the color-to-grayscale alteration, the hands appear exactly the same in the two photos, the jewelry is exactly the same, the foreshortened upward looking perspective is exactly the same (albeit mirror-imaged) in both works. The court found these elements of this visualization of Kevin Garnett to be original to the first artist, and found that the second artist had copied them in violation of the first artist's copyright.

And last, a third set of images:

With these two photographs of an executive apparently staring down from a ledge, you might start by saying, where is the similarity at all? The exhibits are from the case, *Kaplan v. Stock Market Photo.*[6] The artist of the work on the left ("On Top," featuring black shoes) called the work on the right (brown shoes) a copy of the expression of the work on the left. The court was not persuaded. To the extent that the two works have a similar theme—a business executive looking down from a ledge, perhaps preparing to jump—they manage to convey that theme and idea using different imagery, and themes and ideas, in any event, are not copyrightable. The two works have to be examined not as duplicates but at a level of abstraction as depictions of the same subject, a business executive looking down, perhaps contemplating jumping. But this puts the two works directly in the scènes à faire wheelhouse: if you want to convey that the subject is an executive, show him wearing creased and pressed dress pants over polished wingtip shoes. If you want to show that he is a jumper, put the feet on a ledge, and if you want to show the scene from the jumper's perspective, shoot the photograph looking down, over the person's shoes hanging over the ledge, all the way to the street below. All of that adds up to similarity only as to the stock, scènes à faire images used to convey the common subject of the two scenes. It appears obvious that no actual parts of the first image were copied, and the court found no infringement of any copyrightable elements of the first work.

Counterargument: Use of Uncopyrightable Elements

There isn't much hope for the blatant copyist in *Mannion v. Coors*, who appears to have scanned the original image, flipped it, made it grayscale, and cropped it—but the original image shines through in the copy even after all the alterations. But for *Kaplan* or *Satava*, what might have happened if you first compared the two works as a whole before stripping away the parts? Did the second artist capture a single, recognizable whole that is a creative, original composition? Perhaps the *Kaplan* case still remains a case of no infringement. The second artist chose a new set of clothes, different shoes, a different ledge, a different street, and added some original elements—a briefcase and a pigeon. Not so with *Satava*. If we thought of the total concept, look, and feel of Satava's work first, and then Lowry's total concept, look, and feel, we might decide that Lowry had made a pretty blatant copy of Satava's work. Satava might have won on this test. But the abstraction-filtration-comparison test stripped Satava's work to nothing and left nothing for a copyright suit.

Doll Faces Not in Part but in Whole

The total concept, look, and feel test examines the entire composition of the first work as against the entire composition of the second work. If it finds similarities, then the court examines what compositional elements of the two works are similar. It may be that it is the total arrangement and composition of otherwise unoriginal, uncopyrightable parts that has been copied, and an original, creative compilation and arrangement can be copyrighted.

Doll faces illustrate this principle well. Each doll face is made up of some predictable elements—large, widely separated eyes with exaggerated eye lashes; a small, pert nose; bow-shaped lips (as in bow and arrow, not bow on a package); rosy, healthy looking cheeks.

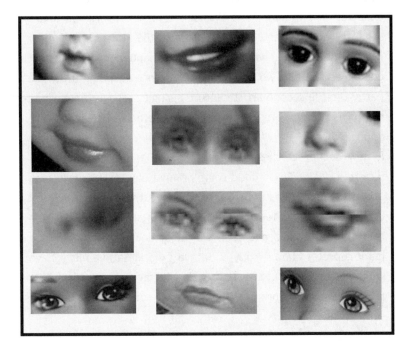

If you add a sufficient quantity of these predictable parts together, you get a recognizable doll face. No one would mistake the combination for that of an actual young girl's face. And yet, even though each doll face has the separate earmarks that in combination make the whole a doll face, each doll's face still can be a unique compilation and arrangement that is copyrightable.

The combination does not have to duplicate another artist's combination. In other words, the separate earmarks may be combined in many different ways, and none of them need copy the combination and arrangement of another doll-maker in order to communicate "doll" to the viewer.

Using the requisite parts of dolls faces in combination also does not automatically add up to a Barbie's doll face. Look closely at the three doll heads here. Two are real Barbies, one is an imposter bought on the streets of an Italian city. Which is the imposter?

If you said, the doll in the middle without much hesitation, that is because Mattel has gone to great lengths to put together a unique combination of otherwise unprotectable features to make a Barbie face. Add standard bow lips to pert nose to healthy cheeks to widely spaced, disproportionately large eyes, with just the right exaggeration of eye liner, brow, and lashes, and you have a Barbie— unmistakably so. Add too much eye liner and clumpy lashes, and you have a cheap counterfeit of Barbie.

Mattel can protect its Barbie compilation from infringement in copyright but the task is made much easier if not absolutely dependent on the court using the total concept, look, and feel test, and not the abstraction-filtration-comparison test. If the abstraction-filtration-comparison test is used, it is likely that the court will strip away the uncopyrightable standard doll face features of Barbie as scènes à faire or merged elements of the idea of the work, similar to what was done to the standard jellyfish elements of Satava's work in the *Satava v. Lowry* case. After stripping away ninety percent of the facial elements of a Barbie doll, it would be hard to imagine what would be left to compare to the facial elements of a competing doll. However, in a real Barbie doll cases, *Mattel Inc. v. Goldberger Doll,*[7] the Second Circuit Court of Appeals applied the total concept, look, and feel test, and evaluated the totality of the Barbie doll to the total concept, look and feel of a competitor's doll, and found that the competitor's doll (Goldberger's "Rockettes doll") infringed Mattel's Barbie doll.

Review and Discussion—
Taking It to the Streets

Now that you have been educated as to the originality and idea-expression requirements of copyright, and the workings of the merger and scènes à faire doctrines, apply this information to the copyrightability of street art. Street art often appropriates the work of others. It may draw on common themes, stock images, and other unoriginal content to make its commentary. Identify some limitations imposed on the potential copyrights over these works of street art by the originality and idea-expression requirements, and the merger and scènes à faire doctrines:

4.1

4.2

4.3

4.4

4.5

Works by Banksy (4.1, 4.2), and Mr. Brainwash (Thierry Guetta) (4.3, 4.4, 4.5).

(See Discussion and Answers on the page that follows.)

Discussion and Answers— Taking It to the Streets	
4.1 London Telephone Box	The Banksy telephone box itself has certain scènes à faire material in it, namely the general appearance of a telephone box and a pick axe. But Banksy, the artist, reconfigured and recreated the box and axe into a totally new work with original content and expression. The overall appearance of the box and the pick axe is now in the form of a crumpled "body" impaled by the axe, and the fake dripping "blood" indicates the violence of the pick axe's interaction with the "body" of the telephone box. This entire arrangement presents creative original material that would be subject to copyright protection.
4.2 Girl Frisking Soldier	Much of this Banksy image has scènes à faire implications: the actual appearance of soldiers, young girls, and rifles; the stock cartoon way of depicting soldiers in uniform and small girls in prim little dresses. Even the particular style and coloration of the dress chosen for the girl is a nostalgic stock image—intentionally so, as Banksy wanted to communicate something ironic in the arrangement of the cartoony, stock images of the girl and the soldier but with the girl frisking the soldier. This creative original juxtaposition of the two subjects of the image creating new meaning and expression for the work as a whole would be subject to copyright protection.

4.3 Warhol as Marilyn Portrait	Thierry Guetta—"Mr. Brainwash"—is piling an irony on top of an irony by depicting a portrait of Warhol in the artistic style of Warhol with hair taken from a familiar image created by Warhol in his Marilyn Monroe series. Warhol's goal was to show the ubiquity of celebrity images, made all the more ubiquitous by his repetition of the images. Here, Guetta puts Warhol himself under Marilyn's hair, making a tongue in cheek comment on Warhol's work. Naturally, Guetta cannot claim a copyright on the actual appearance of Warhol or on any of Warhol's works taken and adapted for this work. At most, this work might have a thin copyright on the total compilation of Warhol's image plus Warhol's distinctive artistic style plus Warhol's Marilyn hair. Guetta will not have even that much to protect if the work is abstracted, filtered, and compared.
4.4 Elvis Don't be Cruel Mashup	Much of this Thierry Guetta image is the black-and-white photographic image of Elvis which is not original or creative when produced by Guetta. The colorful M-16 machine gun and paint splatters are Guetta's addition to the image. Many aspects of the appearance of the gun might be reduced by scènes à faire, but the unnatural, toy-like coloration of the gun would remain. The paint splatters are all Guetta's, and they are copyrightable.

4.5 Tomato Spray Can	Guetta's work again pays homage to Warhol, but "homage" does not produce an original or creative work in copyright terms with regard to the potential rights of the second artist. The shape of the spray can sculpture itself is not copyrightable under the scènes à faire and merger doctrines, and the label is not original and not creative with regard to Guetta's efforts (and this does not take into account other possible intellectual property problems involving trademark and trade dress protections). Campbell's elements on the label are not copyrightable by Guetta (not original or creative). The word "spray" on the label, and maybe the particular design of the paint drip from the nozzle—these are Guetta's creations, and are copyrightable.

---

[1] Although the term "scènes à faire" undeniably is in the French language, the term did not come from France copyright law, but from the opinion of an American federal judge who borrowed this phrase from French literary criticism to express the originality and idea-expression concepts within copyright law that we now label as the scènes à faire doctrine. *See Cain v. Universal Pictures*, 47 F. Supp. 1013, 1017 (S.D Cal. 1942) (Yankwich, D.J.).

[2] *Ets-Hokin v. Skyy Spirits, Inc.*, 225 F.3d 1068 (9th Cir. 2000), and 323 F.3d 763 (9th Cir. 2003).

[3] *Satava v. Lowry*, 323 F.3d 805, 812-13 (9th Cir. 2003).

[4] *Ets-Hokin*, 323 F.3d at 763.

[5] *Mannion v. Coors Brewing Co.*, 377 F. Supp. 2d 444 (S.D.N.Y. 2005).

[6] *Kaplan v. Stock Market Photo Agency, Inc.*, 133 F. Supp. 2d 317 (S.D.N.Y. 2001).

[7] *Mattel, Inc. v. Goldberger Doll Mfg. Co.*, 365 F.3d 133 (2d Cir. 2004).

CHAPTER 5

Utilitarian and Functional Works

The design and functioning of useful articles are excluded from copyright protection. The "utilitarian and functional works" doctrine—also known as the "useful articles" doctrine—is designed to prevent the long term protections of copyright law from attaching to useful articles and creations that have function and utility, as opposed to purely ornamental works or purely expressive works such as literature, music, and the like. The public policy of intellectual property protection in the United States supports the public good first and foremost, and items with utility (clothing, tools, vehicles, appliances) benefit the public when they are made available in large numbers with diverse designs and different price-points. An open and robust level of market competition requires a certain freedom of duplication, replication, emulation, and incremental innovation that is not permissible with copyrighted works under copyright law's derivative works protection.

The two principle areas of intellectual property law, patent and copyright law, are governed by the same "public-first" public policy, and because both patent and copyright law grant a monopoly on the duplication and replication of the things that are protected, patent law, with its relatively short twenty-year term, is given the control over useful, functional articles and functional aspects of articles, while copyright law, with its much longer "lifetime of the author plus seventy years" term, is given sway over non-functional, non-utilitarian, expressive works.

Patents for Utility, Copyrights for Expression

The most important principle to learn regarding copyright's "useful articles" law and policy is that copyright law does not protect innovation and invention of utilitarian items. Patent law is the area of intellectual property law that protects innovation and invention, but the term is far more limited (20 years) than copyright, and the requirements are high. In patent law, you must have a true invention, not anticipated by other works, and not something easily and readily anticipated by others skilled in the art and science of the invention. In copyright, works are supposed to be ornamental and expressive, not useful. If a form has both expressive characteristics and function, the functional aspects will be excluded from the protection of copyright so that these aspects will not be tied up in a copyright monopoly for the life of the creator plus 70 years.

The utilitarian and functional works doctrine seeks to preserve competition and progress in the production of useful articles. By keeping useful, functional works out of copyright protection, the doctrine allows competitors in industry to make useful articles without the fear that the first competitor to design a product will have the right to exclude all others who want to make the same product. Where form follows or leads to function, copyright could tie up a certain form for a term of life plus 70 years. That is a long time for a monopoly on a useful object.

Utility issues come up most often with sculpture. Is the work functional, and if so, is there a way to separate the functional aspects from the non-functional, ornamental, or purely expressive aspects? The separation can be literal and physical (you actually can pull the components apart), or conceptual (if part of the object has creative, original expression that is unrelated to the functioning of the item—e.g., decoration—that you can imagine as a separate original creation). When the functional elements of a work are physically or conceptual separable from the purely expressive elements of the work, then the expressive elements may retain their copyright protection.

Physically Separable Parts

Mazer v. Stein[1] is a United States Supreme Court case that is quite indicative of the way the useful articles doctrine works with regard to physical separation of elements of a work. The case involved the statuettes shown below that were being used by a manufacturer as lamp bases. The question presented by the case was whether the statuette portions of the lamps were copyrightable even though the rest of the lamps were functional.

The high court held that the statuettes themselves were copyrightable because they are physically separable from the lamps. The statuettes did not contribute in any way to the functioning of the lamp *as a lamp* (making it brighter, or improving its illumination or energy-efficiency, for example). Yes, the statuettes hold up the socket, the bulb, and the shade, but that use is fortuitous, and any sturdy object of a certain height could replace the statuettes, and the lamp would still shine just as brightly.

Silk Dresses or Silk Sculptures

Dresses, like other items of clothing, are utilitarian works with useful functions, and they are not copyrightable. If the dress cannot be worn as a dress—for example, it has no openings for the head or arms—then perhaps it is not a "dress" at all; it might be a fabric artwork, a "silk sculpture" for example. But an actual dress raises useful articles issues.

A pattern for a dress, meaning the two-dimensional dress pattern used by a seamstress or dress maker to create the dress, is copyrightable in the form of a dress pattern. What this means is that no one can copy that pattern in its two-dimensional, sheets of paper form.

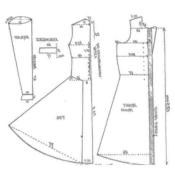  

Because of the useful articles doctrine, a copyright on the dress pattern does not automatically prevent others from using the pattern to create an actual dress. On the one hand, you will not be able to prevent others from making some sorts of dresses based on the pattern to the extent that the process or procedure and other "ideas" of dresses are obtained by studying the pattern, but you might limit them from making an exact copy (again, this is a "derivative work" issue that will be discussed in Chapter 7). The useful, functional parts of the creation—that which makes a dress a dress—will not be protected. They could not be protected under copyright in the original work, so they will not be precluded as a derivative work made by a different person using the pattern.

However, some aspects of the dress design may not be functional, they will be purely decorative or ornamental, and if these appear and could be copied from your pattern, you potentially could prevent those aspects from being copied and made into a derivative work. Fabric decoration, for example, could be protected, as seen in the following designs for fabric created by the author:

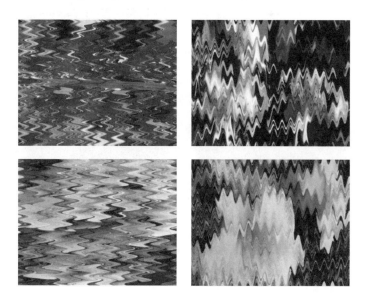

Successful dress designers and dress makers may wish to protect the style, cut, or other distinctive features that tell buyers that this dress is the maker's dress. Unfortunately, that is a good strategy for trademark law, not copyright. Trademark protects such stylistic adornments if they are used as markers of goods in commerce to distinguish the source of the goods from other manufacturers. Dolce Gabbana's buckles and Chanel's necklines and arrangement of buttons most likely could claim this kind of protection. To the extent that the adornments are expressive and completely non-functional, they are candidates for copyright protection much like the fabric decoration discussed above. But the functional parts of the buckle or buttons will not be protected under copyright.

The form and functioning of typeface, most clothing and accessories, lighting fixtures, and household appliances are excluded from copyright by the useful articles doctrine. This is in spite of the fact that designers often produce lamps and other household appliances that are quite beautiful. Decorative elements and ornamentation that have nothing to do with the functioning of the object, but which can be described separately as an original, creative work, can be separated from the functional aspects of the work and receive protection. The separation can be physical, as in *Mazer v. Stein*, or conceptual as described in the problems below.

Conceptual Separation of Decoration

The paintings on the plates are not separable—you cannot detach or scrape them off—but it is fairly plain to see that they have nothing to do with the functioning of the plate *as a plate*. They don't make the plates hold food better, or make them stronger, or more stain-resistant. Thus, as compared to the functional parts of the plates, the paintings and decoration are conceptually separable, and thus could be subject to copyright. The particular paintings and decorations shown above might have other copyright problems—they might be copies of other designs, or otherwise not original to the artist—but the decorations would appear to be copyrightable on the basis of conceptual separation from the utility and functioning of the plates.

If Form Follows from Function, It Is Not Separable

The next lesson of the useful articles doctrine is that when the form of an item (the shape, the design) contributes to its function, it will be difficult for the courts to find that the form is both separable and not utilitarian. The separability of decoration from function is not assumed and it is not automatic. Courts will ponder whether the form of an object actually does make a difference in how it functions. *Esquire, Inc. v. Ringer*[2] is an indicative case for this line of inquiry.

Esquire, Inc. v. Ringer litigated the utility of the design of the Esquire lamp (shown here). At the time it came out, the Esquire lamp was a new look for architectural lighting for pathways and sidewalks. The Esquire people wanted to protect its appearance under copyright law from duplication and derivative copying because the design was not an invention, and no patent protection was available. Esquire had not been using the overall shape of this lamp in commerce as an identifier of the source of the goods (i.e., that this shape of lamp was a mark that the lamp was an Esquire product) long enough to try for trademark protection. The Esquire people did not seek to protect the work's functioning as a lamp—no lamps with lights on either side of a pole and facing down were to be precluded by this copyright. All Esquire wanted to protect was the exact shape of the lamp housing, which Esquire asserted was decorative and not functional.

Nevertheless, the court did not separate the form from the function. To the court's eye, there was no obvious decorative or expressive value to the shape of the work; it read as a lamp from start to finish. The T-design seemed structural and allowed a minimal but sturdy form to hold two lights; you would have a hard time describing the shape of the object without mentioning its function and operation (e.g., "The T-crossbar holds two lights—Oops! I didn't want to mention lights."). Thus, copyright protection was withheld on the basis of functionality.

Three Cheers for Conceptual Separability

While physical separability of decoration from functionality generally presents an easy case, conceptual separability has given the courts a great deal to talk about. In a 2017 United States Supreme Court case, the high court considered the design and appearance of cheerleading uniforms: *Star Athletica, L.L.C. v. Varsity Brands, Inc.*[3] Like Esquire, Inc., before it, Varsity Brands sought to protect the designs of its cheerleading uniforms[4] from duplication and derivative work copying through copyright law because the designs were not an invention suitable for patent protection, and Varsity was not using individual designs as a trademark of the Varsity Brands manufacturing source. Varsity had more than 200 copyright registrations for two-dimensional designs, consisting of various lines, chevrons, and colorful shapes appearing on the surface of the cheerleading uniforms that it designed, manufactured, and sold.

Varsity alleged that defendant Star Athletica infringed Varsity's two-dimensional copyrights by manufacturing cheerleading uniforms incorporating the same two-dimensional designs. Star Athletica alleged that since the functional aspects of clothing (including uniforms) cannot be separated from the design elements that make each article useful, Varsity's designs were not copyrightable. The district court (trial level court) held that a cheerleading uniform is not a cheerleading uniform without stripes, chevrons, etc., and that Varsity's copyrights were therefore invalid because the artistic elements were not physically or conceptually separable from the utilitarian aspects of the uniforms. However, the Sixth Circuit Court of Appeals reversed and remanded the case. The Sixth Circuit court used a hybrid approach to determining conceptual separability, asking (1) is the design a pictorial, graphic, or sculptural work, (2) if so, then is it a design of a useful article, (3) what are the utilitarian aspects of the useful article, (4) can the viewer of the design identify pictorial, graphic, or sculptural features separately from the utilitarian aspects of the useful article, and (5) can the pictorial, graphic, or sculptural features of the design of the useful article exist independently of the utilitarian aspects of the useful article.

On appeal from the Sixth Circuit's opinion, the United States Supreme Court affirmed the Sixth Circuit and held Varsity's designs to be copyrightable. The Supreme Court clarified that: (1) a feature incorporated into the design of a useful article is eligible for copyright protection only if the feature can be perceived as a two- or three-dimensional work of art separate from the useful article, and that it would qualify as a protectable pictorial, graphic, or sculptural work, either on its own or fixed in some other tangible medium of expression, if it were imagined separately from the useful article into which it is incorporated; (2) the arrangements of lines, chevrons, and colorful shapes appearing on surface of cheerleading uniforms could be perceived as two-dimensional works of art separate from the uniforms, and that the arrangements would qualify as protectable pictorial, graphic, or sculptural works eligible for copyright protection as separable features; and (3) the same test is applied to evaluate physical separability and conceptual separability.

Helpful Decoration or Design

The designers and manufacturers of many useful articles will incorporate designs and decorations into their products to make them more desirable and attractive, and therefore more marketable. Competitors will argue that such designs make the items more useful and helpful as the product itself, and argue that this usefulness should be part of the analysis of whether the function of the product benefits from the form or design, and is therefore utilitarian and noncopyrightable.

An example of this situation is seen in the *Home Legend, LLC v. Mannington Mills, Inc.*[5] case. Both Plaintiff Home Legend and Defendant Mannington Mills sell laminated flooring products. Mannington claimed it owned a copyright for its "Glazed Maple" design, but Home Legend, maker of a similar "Distressed Maple Mendocino" design,[6] argued that Mannington's copyright was invalid because Mannington could not obtain copyright protection for a useful article (among other claims). Mannington argued in turn that the décor paper layer of the flooring product was "for all intents and purposes, like putting a painting on the floor," and was therefore copyrightable as a work of art. The trial court held that even though Mannington had obtained a copyright for the 2-D artwork, the 2-D artwork element of the laminate flooring was not separable from the utilitarian aspect of the flooring because the laminate flooring was not marketable if its functional elements were separated from the artistic elements, and conversely, the 2-D artwork would not be marketable if separated from the functional elements of the flooring. However, the circuit court of appeals disagreed, reasoning that the flooring and the décor paper were both physically separable (the décor paper was interchangeable and removable from the flooring) and conceptually separable (the pattern could reasonably be used as wallpaper, a picture frame, or just a piece of art). The court therefore concluded that the defendant's work was sufficiently original and conceptually separable from the utilitarian aspects of the flooring to qualify for copyright protection. Although predating the opinion of the United States Supreme Court in *Varsity Brands*, the outcome in *Home Legend* is supported by the Supreme Court's opinion, because the analysis would come down to whether the maple design could exist separately from the flooring itself as a 2-D pictorial work of art, and the court of appeals answered that question in the affirmative, and therefore the maple design was protectable in copyright.

Distressed Maple Mendocino   Glazed Maple

A similar claim was alleged and litigated in *Inhale, Inc. v. Starbuzz Tobacco, Inc.*[7] This case, too, predates *Varsity Brands*, but the outcome is supported by the later Supreme Court opinion. In *Inhale*, Plaintiff Inhale, Inc. claimed copyright protection for the shape of a hookah water container it registered with the U.S. Copyright Office in 2011. Plaintiff claimed that Defendant Starbuzz sold hookah water containers identical in shape to plaintiff's container.[8] Both plaintiff and defendant agreed that plaintiff's hookah water container is a "useful article," but differed on whether the shape of the bottle is a sculptural feature that can be identified separately from, and is capable of existing independently of, the utilitarian aspects of the container. It is important to note that Inhale's container had the skull and cross-bones design on it, and Starbuzz's container did not; thus, the claim was not about the ornamental design on Inhale's container, but only the shape of the container.

The Ninth Circuit relied on (1) *Ets-Hokin v Skyy Spirits, Inc.*[9] [discussed above in Chapter 4, on scènes à faire and merger], which held that the shape of a vodka bottle was not separable from its utilitarian features, and (2) the Copyright Office's reasoning that an item's distinctive shape does not suggest separability as a separate work of 3-D art, when the shape of the bottle and the shape of any sculptural work of art imagined separately from the bottle would be the same. In both the actual form and the imagined form, *Inhale* would have produced the same useful article, and therefore, the shape of its bottle was not separable and not copyrightable.

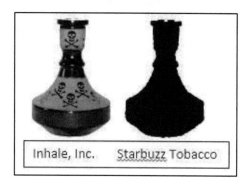

Inhale, Inc.   Starbuzz Tobacco

Review and Discussion—Useful Articles

As a review of your understanding of the workings of the useful articles doctrine, consider the copyrightability of the following objects:

5.1 Baptismal font   5.2 Spray can   5.3 Concept car

What original and creative elements can be separated from the functioning of the object? Can you make a description of these elements without also mentioning the function or operation of the object? Are the elements you listed physically separable or conceptually separable?

(See Discussion and Answers on the page that follows.)

Discussion and Answers—Useful Articles	
5.1 Baptismal font	The decoration on the sides of the font has nothing to do with holding water or dipping things into the water. One could image each of the designs existing as a separate 2-D work of pictorial art. Therefore, the decorative designs are conceptually separable, and copyrightable.
5.2 Spray can	The spray can is functional (or at least it appears to be), but the label and its design are separable, either physically or conceptually. One could image each of the designs existing as a separate 2-D work of pictorial art; in fact, it would exist as a derivative work taken from a rather famous series of works by Andy Warhol. The label is expressive and decorative, and physically or conceptually separable, and therefore, it potentially can be copyrighted. Bonus points if you were thinking, "Yes, but a lot of this work is not original to this artist, it is original to some guy at Campbell's Soup Company many years ago, or at least to Andy Warhol some decades ago." You are right. The creative, original additions to the old Campbell's soup design (i.e., the word, "graffiti"), and at a certain level, the total concept, look, and feel of the assembled arrangement of uncopyrightable parts is all that the second artist could hope to protect with his own, new copyright.

| 5.3 Concept car | The concept car is perhaps the most challenging example. All of the interesting features of an automobile also tend to play a role in the functioning of the car as a car. The distinctive grill opening actually lets air in to cool the engine. The fenders protect the wheels and cover the parts underneath, not to mention channeling the air across and around the vehicle; the seats are seats, the steering wheel steers, the windshield shields the occupants from the wind. Nothing about this car seems ripe for copyright protection. |

---

[1]   *Mazer v. Stein*, 347 U.S. 201 (1954).

[2]   *Esquire, Inc. v. Ringer*, 591 F.2d 796 (D.C. Cir. 1978), *cert. denied*, 440 U.S. 908 (1979).

[3]   *Star Athletica, L.L.C. v. Varsity Brands, Inc.*, 137 S. Ct. 1002, 197 L. Ed. 2d 354 (2017).

[4]   Image: Michael D. Murray, Thumbnail-Sized Excerpts of Exhibits Depicting Varsity Brand Cheerleading Uniform Designs, at issue in *Star Athletica, L.L.C. v. Varsity Brands, Inc.*, 137 S. Ct. 1002 (2017).

[5]   *Home Legend, LLC v. Mannington Mills, Inc.*, 784 F.3d 1404 (11th Cir. 2015)

[6]   Image: Michael D. Murray, Thumbnail-Sized Excerpts of Exhibits Depicting Home Legend's "Distressed Maple Mendocino" design and Mannington Mills' "Glazed Maple" design, at issue in *Home Legend, LLC v. Mannington Mills, Inc.*, 784 F.3d 1404 (11th Cir. 2015).

[7]   *Inhale, Inc. v. Starbuzz Tobacco, Inc.*, 755 F.3d 1038 (9th Cir. 2014).

[8]   Image: Michael D. Murray, Thumbnail-Sized Excerpts of Exhibits Depicting Inhale, Inc.'s and Starbuzz Tobacco's Hookah Water Container Designs, at issue in *Inhale, Inc. v. Starbuzz Tobacco, Inc.*, 755 F.3d 1038 (9th Cir. 2014).

[9]   *Ets-Hokin v. Skyy Spirits, Inc.*, 745 F.2d 1239.

CHAPTER 6

Copyright Term and the Public Domain

Copyright is intended to have a limited term. The Founding Fathers wrote a requirement into the Constitution, Article I, Section 8, Clause 8, to provide that copyright is intended:

> To promote the Progress of Science and useful Arts, by securing **for limited Times** to Authors and Inventors the exclusive Right to their respective Writings and Discoveries . . . . (emphasis supplied).

Therefore, copyright monopolies are supposed to have a limited time frame. But Congress sets the terms, and Congress can be lobbied. And across the two centuries of its existence, Congress periodically changed the terms, usually to extend the term of protection, or provide for successive, renewal terms. The latest, greatest term extension was the Sono Bono Copyright Term Extension Act of 1998, in which the major studios and entertainment giants, led by Disney, rallied around the deceased pop singer and congressman, Sonny Bono, of Sonny and Cher fame, and managed to get Congress to extend corporate-owned copyright terms to keep

Mickey Mouse and many other valuable intellectual properties from falling into the public domain.

Copyright terms of protection are not exceedingly complicated, but there are a lot of categories to keep track of, and, as mentioned above, Congress has a habit of prolonging the terms, so take a grain of salt with you as you study this chart of copyright terms:

CREATION DATE OF WORK	INITIATION OF PROTECTION	DURATION
After Jan. 1, 1978	When work is fixed in tangible medium of expression	Life + 70 years. [Jointly created works are measured by life of longest living coauthor] If the work is of corporate authorship (including works made for hire, anonymous, and pseudonymous works), the duration is the shorter of 95 years from publication, or 120 years from creation

CREATION DATE OF WORK	INITIATION OF PROTECTION	DURATION
Before 1963	When published with notice [If no notice was given, the work has entered the public domain]	28 years, and it could have been renewed for 47 years and extended by law another 20 years for a total renewal of 67 years. [If not renewed, it is now in the public domain]
From 1964–1977	When published with notice [If no notice was given, the work has entered the public domain]	28 years, now automatically extended by law another renewal term of 67 years
Before Jan. 1, 1978 but not published	Jan. 1, 1978, the effective date of the 1976 Act which eliminated common law copyright	Life + 70 years or Dec. 31, 2002, whichever is greater
Before Jan. 1, 1978 but published between then and Dec. 31, 2002	Jan. 1, 1978, the effective date of the 1976 Act which eliminated common law copyright	Life + 70 years or Dec. 31, 2047, whichever is greater

CREATION DATE OF WORK	INITIATION OF PROTECTION	DURATION
After Jan. 1, 1978 and before Mar. 1, 1989 (eff. date of Berne Convention Impl. Act)	When work is fixed in tangible medium of expression, but notice not given	Under § 405, registration must be made within five years of creation to retain copyright term of Life + 70 years

What this chart means is that currently the default term for published and unpublished works created and fixed in a tangible medium by an author after 1977 and owned by the author or another individual, is the life of the author plus 70 years. For corporate-owned works, anonymous works, or works made for hire (these classifications are further explained in Chapter 8 "Works Made for Hire and Copyright Ownership") created after 1977, the term is 95 years from the date of publication or 120 years from the date of creation, whichever expires first. These terms are subject to change because Congress might act to extend the terms, as it did for the 1923–1977 published works.

The group of 1923–1977 published works is the tricky category. For *published* works (the kind you are most likely to encounter in life) that were published and copyright registered between 1923 and 1977, the term is set to expire on Jan. 1, 2019, for the earliest (1923) works, and then each year thereafter, another year of published works will fall into the public domain. The current plan is to allow these works a 95 year term (note that you get the full 95th year, through Dec. 31, regardless of in what part of the year the work was published). Therefore, 1924 works expire on Jan. 1, 2020,

1925 works expire on Jan. 1, 2021, and so on. That is, unless Congress extends these terms again.

Unpublished works were not the concern of copyright until 1977. If you come across an unpublished work from the 1923-1977 time period, you had better consult an attorney to find out what you might do with it. In this time period, publication usually meant registration with the Library of Congress. It did not mean revealed, printed, or broadcasted to the world.

Pre-1923 works were not rescued by Congress. Apparently, Disney and the film and entertainment industry didn't have much to protect in the pre-1923 time period, so they left it alone when they lobbied Congress to extend the terms.

The following works are no longer protected by copyright in the United States—they are in the public domain (discussed below):

- All works published in the U.S. before 1923

- All works published with a copyright notice from 1923 through 1963 whose owners did not seek a copyright renewal when the initial term expired

- All works published without a copyright notice from 1923 through 1977

- All works published without a copyright notice from 1978 through March 1, 1989, and without subsequent registration within 5 years.

The **public domain** is the legal term for all the created, authored material that no longer is subject to copyright protection. It used to be that works fell into the public domain by accident—being published without a copyright notice, for example—and others just timed out. These days, authors sometimes donate (or dedicate) a work to the public domain as a gesture of good will and in the spirit that works should be free for copying, exploitation, and further distribution.

Works in the public domain are free for the taking. You can copy them or reprint and republish them. You can build on them, change them, do what you want with them. All is permitted. Note that if you reproduce or republish public domain works, you will not get a new copyright on the works. If you add to them, you will only get a copyright on that which you added.

If you want a new copyright on a work that used to be public domain or which contains public domain material, you have to follow copyright's requirements and do something to the work that makes it original to you that is conceived of and created by you. And for public domain content, the change has to be substantial and material. You cannot just put a new cover on it or change the title. Copyright wants a new work with new expression. Note, too, that the copyright you obtain only runs forward on the creative, original part or arrangement that you added. The public domain content that you did not alter in a substantial material way remains public domain material.

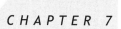

CHAPTER 7

Derivative Works

Copyright precludes the unauthorized copying of original creations whose expressions are fixed in a tangible media, but that is not all it precludes. Copyright also precludes others from adapting the content of an original work for their own purposes. The derivative works right gives copyright owners the right to preclude exact, direct, and verbatim copies of their work, and also adaptations, translations, and extensions of the work in new works or new media.

The law defines derivative works rather broadly:

> A "derivative work" is a work based upon one or more preexisting works, such as a translation, musical arrangement, dramatization, fictionalization, motion picture version, sound recording, art reproduction, abridgment, condensation, *or any other form in which a work may be recast, transformed, or adapted.* A work consisting of editorial revisions, annotations, elaborations, or other modifications which, as a whole, represent an original work of authorship, is a "derivative work."[1]

Thus, the copyright holder controls the original and those works that can be made that incorporate the original work's expressive, communicative potential (subject, of course, to originality, idea-expression, merger, and scènes à faire limitations). Basically, any subsequent work that incorporates part of the expression of the original work such that this expression shines through in the new work can qualify as a derivative work. And the original copyright owner can authorize or preclude the creation of such works.

The law is clear that you don't get a new copyright (and a new copyright term) over the preexisting copyrighted work you own and control when you adapt it and reuse it for a new creation. Only the newly added original and creative material gets a new copyright running from the new creation date. Thus, if an author prepares a new edition of an existing text, she only gets a new copyright on the newly added, edited, or updated material. The other material still in the book from the first edition retains the same copyright and term from the original edition.

The derivative works right was designed with fairness to the original creator in mind, but it is not easy to apply in practice. A famous twentieth century jurist, Judge Learned Hand, characterized the problem in *Nichols v. Universal Pictures Corp.*[2] as arising from the fact that an idea as opposed to the expression of the idea in literature can be manipulated by viewing the interest protected by copyright at differing levels of abstraction.[3] If protection is limited to the words as they appear on the page—a strictly literal application of the term "expression"—the protection for original "Writings" envisioned by the Constitution would be considerably thin—unfairly thin, in fact. A new author could imitate the plot, character types, exposition, conflict, resolution, and all other original elements of a novel so long as she changed the wording. All of us could take a crack at writing new Harry Potter novels extending the characters types and situations of the books past the last chapter of the seven books written by J.K. Rowling, and hope not only for fame but for copyrightable works that we can sell, exploit, and make money on.

But if copyright protection extends to the full range of derivative works that might be expressed by the author arising from the author's fleshing out of an "idea" in literature, then an author could claim property rights to an entire genre. As discussed above, Edgar Allan Poe or Wilkie Collins could have captured the mystery and crime novel genre with the publication of a single story; the innovators of the first reality television show, *Survivor*, might have deprived the public of *The Amazing Race*, *Fear Factor*, *Big Brother*, or even *Temptation Island*. This is the point where, in theory, the idea-expression doctrine and its companions of merger and scènes à faire impose the originality requirement's limitations on derivative works. I say, *in theory*, because the application is inexact and challenging.

The *Nichols* case is an example of a challenging analysis. The case involved two literary works, a stage play called *Abie's Irish Rose* by Anne Nichols, and a screenplay called *The Cohens and Kellys*, which were alleged to be substantially similar.

It is quite common for a stage play to be adapted into a screenplay, or vice versa, so the court wrestled with the concept of whether the second work—the screenplay—was an unauthorized derivative of the first work. Note that there was no allegation that actual scenes or actual text were copied from the first work into the second, but Judge Hand observed that, "It is of course essential to any protection of literary property, whether at common-law or under the statute, that the right cannot be limited literally to the text, else a plagiarist would escape by immaterial variations."[4]

The first work involved a Jewish widower whose son secretly married an Irish Catholic girl whose widower father was as against the union as the Jewish father was. Eventually, the two fathers reconcile in order to rejoin the company of their respective children and grandchildren. The second work involved a Jewish family who lived in a state of animosity with their neighbors, an Irish Catholic family. The only family members not engaged in the quarrel from the fathers to the mothers (who are present and accounted for), to young children and family pets, were the daughter of the Jewish family and the son of the Irish family, who, as you may have guessed, secretly marry. Further conflict is introduced when the Jewish father inherits a sizeable sum of money, but later learns that the proper legatee is the Irish father, and in turning over the money, he prompts an unlikely friendship and partnership between the two fathers.

Judge Hand noted that,

> [W]hen the plagiarist does not take out a block in suit, but an abstract of the whole, decision is more troublesome. Upon any work, and especially upon a play, a great number of patterns of increasing generality will fit equally well, as more and more of the incident is left out. The last may perhaps be no more than the most general statement of what the play is about, and at times might

consist only of its title; but there is a point in this series of abstractions where they are no longer protected, since otherwise the playwright could prevent the use of his "ideas," to which, apart from their expression, his property is never extended. [citation omitted] Nobody has ever been able to fix that boundary, and nobody ever can.[5]

If a bona fide legal genius such as Learned Hand says nobody can fix a boundary, he is probably right. But legal determinations must be made.

The opinion declared that stealing lines or scenes, or stealing specific characters from a work may be actionable if it is a substantial taking, but the comparison of the similarity of two plots and storylines requires examination of the lowest level of abstraction it takes to find the two works to be the same; if the works are only similar at a high level of abstraction, it will be less likely that their similarity will constitute actionable infringement. For example, the two works at issue in *Nichols* may be abstracted as follows (starting with a high level of abstraction and working downward):

- two works about two men with children;

- two works about two men whose children marry;

- two works about two men whose children marry causing the men grief and anger;

- two works about two men whose children marry in secret causing the men grief and anger;

- two works about two men from different religions whose children marry in secret causing the men grief and anger because of their religious differences;

- two works about two men from different religions whose children marry in secret causing the men grief and anger because of their religious differences but who reconcile in the end;

- two works about a Jewish man and an Irish Catholic man whose children marry in secret causing them grief and anger because of their religious differences but who reconcile in the end;

and so on.

If the level of abstraction at which the works share the most similarities mainly involves the level of ideas (e.g., the idea of pig-headed men who cannot get along because of religious differences; the idea of men who overcome petty religious differences in favor of stronger values), or generalities (e.g., problems of marriages of two people from different religions; the situation of marriages that cause animosity in families but later produce a kind of coexistence), or repeats plot devices and stock themes common to many works (e.g., star-crossed lovers; feuding families brought together by a marriage of defectors; fathers who compromise because of love of children or grandchildren), then the works are similar at a level at which the first author cannot claim protection. The abstraction of two literary works for comparison of the plot and storyline must not result in a pattern of similarity that has eliminated so many disparate details of the works that the remaining similarities are simply plot ideas, stock themes, or common character types interacting in predictable ways, and which are precluded from protection by the idea-expression doctrine or the limitations of merger and scènes à faire. This is the level of abstraction where Judge Hand found the two works in *Nichols*, and he rejected the claim for infringement.

The process of abstraction and comparison described in *Nichols* works well in literary works where individual authors, all using a common language (English), may discuss a common theme or plot device or character-type or flesh out a familiar scene or stock image. In such instances, all literary works will share commonalities if they share a common idea but not elements that are original to one author. The idea and the expression of the idea will merge in a literary sense as the idea itself captures the several words and phrases necessary to communicate the idea in writing. Judge Hand recognized that it is prudent to declare such plot ideas, character-types, familiar scenes, and stock images as part of the public domain, available to all authors who wish to embody the idea or scene in their own work. Thus, his decision is the grandfather of both the merger doctrine and the scènes à faire doctrine.

Many allegations of infringement pertain to the alleged creation of unauthorized derivative works. In other words, it is somewhat unusual for a plagiarist to boldly copy verbatim the exact work of another and attempt to pass it off as his own. What is more likely is that a portion of the work, or a close abstraction and adaption of the work is performed, leaving the need to sort out the two works to determine what has been copied, and whether what has been copied was originally protected copyrightable material.

Review and Discussion—Derivative Works

7.1   London Bus & Parliament

As a review of your understanding of the workings of the derivative works doctrine, evaluate the following pair of works. Try to determine if the image on the right appears to be an unauthorized derivative work of the image on the left that might infringe the copyright of the image on the left.

Was the Fielder photo (left) infringed by the Houghton photo (right) after the application of the originality, idea-expression, scènes à faire, and merger doctrines? What protected elements may have been copied?

(See Discussion and Answers on the page that follows.)

Discussion and Answers—Derivative Works

7.1 London Bus & Parliament	The London Bus and Parliament pictures present a difficult analysis under the law. The pictures fall neatly between exactly what should be prevented as a derivative work, and exactly what should be preserved as a stock image of London. The appearance of Parliament, Westminster Bridge, and a typical double-decker bus are standard depictions of a London scene, and therefore are scènes à faire, and not copyrightable. It may not be apparent in the grayscale printing of this book, but the bus in both photographs is red, and rest of the cityscape in both photographs is grayscale. The idea of showing a bus in red while everything else remains in grayscale seems to fit the definition of a merged idea—there is only one way to show a red bus on grayscale image: by doing it. But stripping the two parts leaves nothing in the first image except the exact totality of the image, precluding only a near exact duplicate, which the second image is not. That seems like a harsh outcome. Perhaps under a total concept, look, and feel analysis the total idea of a particular shot of a bus in a certain shade of red and a particular depiction of Parliament in grayscale on a white sky is protectable, and the second image does capture a lot of the total concept, look, and feel of the first image.

[1]   17 U.S.C. § 101 (emphasis added).

[2]   *Nichols v. Universal Pictures Corp.*, 45 F.2d 119 (2d Cir. 1930).

[3]   This section draws heavily from Michael D. Murray, *Copyright, Originality, and the End of the Scènes à Faire and Merger Doctrines for Visual Works*, 58 BAYLOR L. REV. 779, 786-91 (2006).

[4]   *Id.* at 121.

[5]   *Id.*

CHAPTER 8

Works Made for Hire and Copyright Ownership

The traditional and "Romantic" conception of authorship in literature and the arts is for a single author to toil and produce a work for her own ownership and control. In this conception, the individual author or artist owns the copyright over the work she conceived of and created, and makes the decisions about its exploitation through duplication and derivatives.

The world of arts, music, publishing, and entertainment in contemporary times is much more corporate than this Romantic notion of authorship. Many works are created by authors and artists at the instance, direction, and control of others—corporations, record labels, studios and production companies, media companies, and entertainment giants. Many works are created by teams of authors, each playing a role, each contributing to a work that is a unified whole, but which is the product of collective creative effort.

Works made for hire is a term for a work prepared by one person (the author or artist) but owned by another (the owner). This separation of author and owner has certain consequences in the law, the most obvious of which is that the author does not control how the creation is going to be used, exploited, published, and displayed, or what derivative works are going to be created from the original. In the modern world, most successful authors and artists have given up all or a large part of the control of their works to others, making an awareness of work made for hire rules essential for both authors and employers.

Works Created by Employees

The simplest and most common work for hire situation is that of an employee who works for an employer in a creative capacity. 17 U.S.C. § 101's definition of a "work made for hire" begins with:

> (1)   a work prepared by an employee within the scope of his or her employment

As noted in section 101, in order for creative work to be subject to work made for hire status, the creative work must be done within the "scope of employment," which means:

- The work is the kind of activity the employee is employed to perform;

- The work occurs substantially within the authorized time and space limits; and

- The work is actuated, at least in part, by a purpose to serve the master

In other words, the works of the employee artist belong to the employer if they are the kind of works the employee was hired to produce, and they were in fact produced while "on the job" in terms of time, space, and a motivation to produce work for the employer. The time, space, and motivation part might require some factual background on a case-by-case basis because some employees work from home at odd hours, and others do work for the employer while still maintaining a creative business on the side, which both the employer and the employee know about, and whose products are not the property of the employer.

Contractual Works

The second path to work made for hire status for a creative work is the situation where a person or entity enters into a contract with an independent contractor that states in writing that the work is to be a "work made for hire," and that is signed and entered into before the work is completed. However, this option is limited to a few key areas of creative activity.

Section 101 of the Copyright Act states that this "contractual work" version of a work made for hire applies to:

> (2)   a work specially ordered or commissioned for use as a contribution to a collective work, as a part of a motion picture or other audiovisual work, as a translation, as a supplementary work, as a compilation, as an instructional text, as a test, as answer material for a test, or as an atlas, if the parties expressly agree in a written instrument signed by them that the work shall be considered a work made for hire. For the purpose of the foregoing sentence, a "supplementary work" is a work prepared for publication as a secondary adjunct to a work by another author for the purpose of introducing, concluding, illustrating, explaining, revising, commenting upon, or assisting in the use of the other work, such as forewords, afterwords, pictorial illustrations, maps, charts, tables, editorial notes, musical arrangements, answer material for tests, bibliographies, appendixes, and indexes, and an "instructional text" is a literary, pictorial, or graphic work prepared for publication and with the purpose of use in systematic instructional activities.

Section 101's "work made for hire" definition part 2 presents a significant limitation on the kinds of works that may be made subject to the terms of a contract for creation that contains a work made for hire term. True, one category of collective work mentioned in part 2 is "motion pictures or other audiovisual works," so it contains television and movie production, which is an enormous and lucrative area of the arts and entertainment world. But the remaining categories are fairly narrow—translations; supplements to other works, such as illustrations, indices, forewords, afterwords, maps, charts, tables, and graphs for books; and instructional and educational works. The important takeaway is that not every kind of creative endeavor can be shoe-horned into work made by hire status by a contract with a work made for hire term.

Determining Employee vs. Independent Contractor Status

Because the two categories of work made for hire status—employee-produced works, and contractual works—are limited, and because the works produced in these endeavors are so valuable, figuring out whether the person who is working for you on a creative endeavor is an **employee** or an **independent contractor** is a serious concern for copyright law. With employees, the determination of who owns the copyright is fairly straightforward: you must determine whether the work was created within the scope of the employment. After that it is clear that the employer owns the copyright to the work and not the employee. But getting to that question requires you to be sure that the person is in fact an employee and not an independent contractor.

Independent contractors are persons who are not employees but are working for the employer on a piecemeal, special arrangement by agreement between both parties (i.e., by a contract). That does not sound all that different from a layperson's conception of an employee, but because of the work for hire rules, we must make distinctions, sometimes very fine distinctions, to sort the independent contractors from employees through the common law agency test. The goal of the test is to differentiate employees from independent contractors based on a list of traditional agency principles; agency is a legal term for persons who act on your behalf, so the term agency covers both employees and independent contractors. However, the term carries weight in copyright because the work of "employees" always is subject to work made for hire status, but the copyright to the work of independent contractor only belongs to the employer if the work is in one of the limited section 101 part 2 categories *and* is produced under a contract that contains the required "work made for hire" term.

There are no hard and fast rules for who is an employee and who is an independent contractor under the common law agency test; instead there are a list of criteria that can cause the evaluation to lean toward one status or the other:

If employer has this right . . .	Then the relationship leans toward . . .
Right to control the manner and means of production— hours of work, time for completion, order and nature of work	Employer-Employee
Artist sets hours of work, time for completion, order and nature of work	Employer-Independent Contractor
Work must be done at employer's site	Employer-Employee

If employer has this right . . .	Then the relationship leans toward . . .
Work is done at artist's studio or home	Employer-Independent Contractor
Employer supplies tools, materials, equipment	Employer-Employee
Artist supplies tools, materials, equipment	Employer-Independent Contractor
Artist paid a salary	Employer-Employee
Artist paid a one-time fee	Employer-Independent Contractor
Artist paid on commission	Inconclusive. Could go either way
Employer has right to assign more work to artist	Employer-Employee (unless contract terms explain this another way)
Employer pays employee benefits or takes care of Social Security, FICA, and payroll tax withholding	**Employer-Employee.** This is a hugely important factor, the mother of all factors. If the employer is doing this, you can bet the court will find an employer-employee relationship no matter what the above factors might argue for or against.

There might be other factors to weigh in the determination, but as noted in the last entry of the table above, remember to look for the 500lb. gorilla factor: If the employer pays employee benefits or withholds Social Security, FICA, and payroll taxes, the artist is going to be determined to be an employee, and all works produced within the scope of the employment will belong to the employer. This works the other way, too—if the artist takes care of her own taxes and withholding, this is a huge factor in finding her a self-employed independent contractor who happens to have a project with the employer.

Avoid Work Made for Hire Questions—Just Buy the Copyright

If you are not sure of a worker's status, and you want to own the copyright to the work without question, whether the analysis turns toward independent contractor status rather than employee status, then there is a simple solution: just buy the copyright. Copyrights can be transferred from one person to another by a sale or assignment. A contract to sell, license, or assign a copyright does not have anything to do with the parties' employment status any more than a contract to purchase a used car would have anything to do with the buyer's and seller's employment status. An employer who has her doubts about the common law agency status of a worker should contract with the worker separately to purchase not only the works she produces but also the copyrights to the works. The two are separate—the work and the copyright to the work, as discussed below. If you separately buy the copyright, you'll own and control it and need never worry over the common law agency test. You can insert this purchase provision in your original contract with the contractor or in a separate agreement. A purchase agreement will take the guesswork out of who owns the copyright to the work produced in the arrangement.

Copyright Ownership

There are three kinds of copyright ownership: sole ownership, joint ownership, and works made for hire. The copyright law states that by default, the "author" is the initial copyright owner at creation. An exception is category 3 of ownership, works made for hire, discussed above. In addition, copyrights can be transferred, which is referred to as a sale, assignment, and transfer. (To make it sound legalistic, use all three terms in your agreement to sell or purchase a copyright). The owner or transferee may be a person, or a business, or a corporation.

Joint owners agree in advance to contribute expression to a unitary whole, then they become joint owners of the whole. Each joint owner can license, copy, make derivative works, or otherwise exploit the content of the whole; the joint owner is not limited to licensing or copying just the parts the joint owner contributed to the whole, but the joint owner must divide any profits he makes on this venture with the other joint owner(s).

Note that copyright theory in the United States separates a work (the item) from its copyright (the right to copy or make derivative works from the original work). Thus, you can sell a work—a painting, for example—without selling, transferring, or assigning the copyright over the original creation embodied in the painting. This means you retain the control over who, if anyone, gets to copy the painting or make derivative works from the painting. The purchaser of the painting does not have this right unless you sell him the copyright along with the painting.

Note, too, that this is a new innovation in United States copyright law since 1977. 1977 refers to the effective date of the 1976 Copyright Act that overhauled the whole United States copyright code. Before 1977, copyright to works were *presumed* to transfer to the purchasers of the works. If you bought a painting, you also bought the copyright to the painting; or so went the presumption. You could rebut the presumption by agreement—inserting a clause in the sales agreement to the effect that, "In this sale of the painting, buyer will *not* receive the copyright to the painting"—but you had to do something affirmative to rebut the presumption. Since 1977, the opposite presumption is made, that the copyright to the work did *not* transfer to the purchaser of the work *unless* the two agreed to include the copyright in the sale.

(A word to the wise: if you encounter any artists who sold works in the pre-1977 time frame, please break the news to them gently that they probably transferred the copyrights to their works to the purchasers of their works, unless they affirmatively wrote the copyright transfer out of the sales agreement. Finding out that these copyrights are gone tends to make these artists freak out a little).

Review and Discussion—Works Made for Hire

8.1 Sara's Portraits

Consider the employment arrangement between Sara and her employer and determine whether Sara is likely to be found to be an employee or an independent contractor:

Sara paints portraits for Sargent Whistler LLC (SW), a commercial studio that takes commissions for painted portraits and assigns them to a stable of artists who have agreed to work 20-30 hours a week for SW. Sara receives 20% of the commission fees for each portrait she paints for SW. SW routinely withholds income taxes, FICA, and state payroll taxes from her payments. SW provides no health insurance, retirement plan, or any other employee benefit to Sara and the other artists working for SW. SW has a large studio where many of the artists work, but Sara prefers the lighting and work space at her own home, and so she routinely performs her work at home with the knowledge and consent of SW. SW supplies paint, thinners and painting media, and canvases to its artists but not their palates, brushes, knives, or other painting tools and cleaning supplies. In any event, Sara prefers to select her own paints and so she rarely uses the paint supplied by SW, again with the knowledge and consent of SW. Sara, instead, takes a tax write-off for the supplies she expends in her work with SW in the years she earns enough to owe income tax. Sara also accepts her own commissions for portrait work and performs work on those projects in the same place as she does her work for SW; given that the portraits are in oil with its prolonged drying time, Sara often has two or three works in progress for SW sitting in her home studio alongside two or three projects for her own private commissions. Sara has never signed any contract or agreement mentioning ownership of the copyright for works she creates for SW's customers.

Who owns the copyright over works Sara has created for SW's customers?

(See Discussion and Answers on the page that follows.)

Discussion and Answers— Works Made for Hire	
8.1 Sara's Portraits	Is Sara an employee of Sargent Whistler (SW)? There are numerous factors that would weigh on the decision, but one of them is the most important factor—taxes withheld. The factors for Sara would weigh in as follows: • Works on commission—more contractor than employee • Own tools, mounts, paint, and supplies (but they offered her some to use)—more contractor than employee • Works at her home, at her own pace—more contractor than employee • Works on series of projects assigned by her boss for the benefit of the boss—more employee than contractor But there are the taxes: • Taxes withheld—leans the case heavily toward employee, not contractor. Because of the last factor, most likely a court would find that Sara is an employee, and SW owns the works produced by Sara within the scope of their employment agreement.

CHAPTER 9

Fair Uses

I have written many times about fair use, and have lectured for almost two decades to law students and Master of Fine Arts graduate students about its requirements. I have siblings and nieces and nephews who, like me, are artists—there are three painters, two movie makers, and a photographer within my family—and we all face fair use issues on a professional level. Copyright fair use is a challenging topic. As an attorney, sometimes I feel like I am on an endless trudge up a slippery slope of changing fair use law. However, there is a bright side about fair use that I communicate to the practitioners and future lawyers I speak to: copyright fair use law is almost guaranteed to supply full employment for copyright lawyers for the foreseeable future. Fair use is the conundrum of conundrums for creative persons and their lawyers. What is fair, what is not, and what is too close to call makes the selection and use of copyrighted material a harrowing experience for anyone working in the arts, entertainment, recording, and creative industries.

Although my opening to this chapter might be viewed by some as pessimistic, I hasten to change the tone by pointing out that there are some black letter principles about fair use that all readers should know, and there are questions in the area for which there are good, firm answers. The remaining fair use questions present a pleasant challenge and lots of room for lawyering and advocacy. There are constitutional First Amendment issues here, and plenty of opportunities to weave the facts of situations into persuasive narratives using verbal and visual rhetoric. Therefore, there is plenty of grist for the mill of this chapter. It happens to be the longest chapter in this book.

Fair use is an honorable, public policy-driven, First Amendment-guaranteed right. Fair use should be understood so that it can be enjoyed by all. Those who know can make their copies and use them fairly; those who don't will know that they are running the risk and are subject to the consequences. Unfortunately, in an effort to be fair to all sides of this issue—the owners of copyrights, the potential consumers of copyrighted works, the potential fair users of copyrighted content, and to the public at large who would like to be enriched and educated by new works—the law has contrived a full-bodied set of rules and criteria that are very complicated and whose operation is difficult to predict. For that reason, do not be surprised if you or others you deal with, even copyright lawyers, cannot give you a completely definitive, straight up Yes-No answer to many fair use questions. At best, copyright lawyers can make educated predictions, and at worst, educated guesses. But knowledge is power, and educated predictions and guesses are better than ignorant predictions, or simply avoiding the issues altogether by forced abstinence from all copying. Therefore, it is a worthy endeavor to study this beast of the law known as copyright fair use.

Why Is There a Fair Use Escape Hatch Built into Copyright Law?

After reading eight chapters about how the law has tightened the screws and bolted shut the doors and windows against unauthorized copying of original, creative works, you may be wondering why the law built in a rather significant escape hatch for would-be copyists. The answer lies in the public policy of copyright protection: copyright must benefit the public, and members of the public benefit from expansive opportunities to both express themselves and consume the expression of others. When copyright builds walls around content, it excludes the public from free, unrestrained repetition and repurposing of protected expression. Add to this equation the First Amendment public policy that protects and encourages open, robust, unfettered expression in this country, and you arrive at the answer: fair use becomes the public's safety valve or escape hatch from copyright monopoly protection.

A prohibition on copying is a prohibition on a certain form of expression, that of repeating, repurposing, or redistributing another person's expression. This is a form of censorship, a restraint on speech and expression. The form of expression restrained by copyright is held to be valuable because it allows others to repeat and redistribute news and social criticism, it provides an outlet for disgruntled voices, and it can enable self-actualization through identification and repurposing of other's speech.

Copyright is a constitutionally mandated right—it is in the original constitution, Article I, Section 8, Clause 8: copyrights (and patents) are protected "To promote the Progress of Science and useful Arts, by securing for limited Times to Authors and Inventors the exclusive Right to their respective Writings and Discoveries[.]" But the First Amendment also provides constitutionally recognized rights, and although it is an amendment, it is the first of the amendments added in 1791 to secure civil rights to citizens, and it has significant clout.

The First Amendment states, "Congress shall make no law . . . abridging the freedom of speech[.]" In order to respect the two constitutional rights without one swallowing the other, the courts developed the idea-expression distinction and the concept of fair use in copyright law.

A fair use exception has been included in copyright law for as long as there has been recognizable copyright law. It was including in the English copyright law of the eighteenth century (the Statute of Anne[1]). It was adopted into American copyright law in the early nineteenth century.[2] Today, fair use law reflects the codification of section 107 of the 1976 Copyright Act that provides four criteria that are to be balanced in a case-by-case analysis of the facts and situation of the dispute. (Note that balancing and case-by-case analysis are code words for lawyers that mean no one is going to be able to give you a straight up Yes-No answer on a fair use question, but we'll charge you for an educated prediction or guess anyway).

The fair use provision of the 1976 Copyright Act, 17 U.S.C. § 107, states,

> [T]he fair use of a copyrighted work . . . for purposes such as criticism, comment, news reporting, teaching (including multiple copies for classroom use), scholarship, or research, is not an infringement of copyright. In determining whether the use made of a work in any particular case is a fair use the factors to be considered shall include—
>
> > (1) the purpose and character of the use, including whether such use is of a commercial nature or is for nonprofit educational purposes;
> >
> > (2) the nature of the copyrighted work;

(3) the amount and substantiality of the portion used in relation to the copyrighted work as a whole; and

(4) the effect of the use upon the potential market for or value of the copyrighted work.

The fact that a work is unpublished shall not itself bar a finding of fair use if such finding is made upon consideration of all the above factors.

The fair use provision allows expressions that involve the copying of existing, copyrighted works as long as they serve a public policy purpose that approaches the public policy purpose for which we granted a copyright in the first place. In other words, the use must benefit the public with something valuable—such as criticism, comment, news reporting, teaching, scholarship, or research. A use that is largely self-serving and commercially motivated will rarely be designated as fair unless the benefits it brings to the public are so great that the law excuses the selfishness and money-grubbing.

In some instances, the fair use evaluation is fairly straightforward:

- a newspaper can review a play and quote (i.e., copy) some of the dialogue in its review;

- an art critic can explain what she doesn't like about a painting, and show (i.e., copy) a portion of the painting to illustrate what she is talking about;

- a teacher can make photocopies of two pages from a ten page article and pass them out to her class for a lecture and class discussion (but it is a very good idea to collect them back when the discussion is finished);

- a search engine can make thumbnail copies of visual works to illustrate the links to the actual visual works on the internet in the process of providing results to an image search query.

In some cases, it is equally evident what can be predicted to be an *unfair* use:

- a teacher's copying of an entire book and passing it out to her students so she and they all can avoid the cost of purchasing the book is not fair use;

- a news magazine reprinting the most important part of an unpublished biography in an effort to scoop the competition is not fair use;

- downloading copyrighted MP3 music just because you prefer not paying for it is not fair use;

- copying just about any portion of a copyrighted sound recording and using it in another sound recording without permission is held not to be fair;

- any attempt at copying that primarily benefits the copyist by saving them time, effort, and money, as in saving them the drudgery of thinking up something new, is generally going to be evaluated as unfair.

Everything has its limits. You can see from the bullet points in the above list that even educational classroom uses are not categorically immune from infringement, nor is news reporting, and comment and criticism must be handled with care and attention to all of the factors, not just the purpose and character of the use.

Classic Fair Uses Under Section 107

As mentioned above, fair use exceptions have been around for as long as copyright law. Over the years, the factors that tend to make uses fair or unfair were adopted and explained, and some uses were recognized over and over again as being fair. The process came to a head with the passage of Section 107 and the four factors used to evaluate fair uses that are quoted above: (1) purpose and character of the use, (2) nature of the original work, (3) amount taken, and (4) effect on the market for the original.

The 1994 Supreme Court case of *Campbell v. Acuff-Rose*[3] brought together the doctrine and interpretive principles of fair use that both predate and follow the section 107 factors. The Supreme Court said that the factors are to be balanced against each other. No single factor is the key factor anymore (note that commercial vs. noncommercial uses used to be the key factor; now it is just one of the factors). A bad score on one factor can be balanced by a better score on another. And the evaluation is to be made on a case-by-case basis taking all of the factors and circumstances of the case into account.

After *Campbell*, the courts set about on their case-by-case determinations, and grew a body of law from which to assess the weight and interaction of the four section 107 fair use factors. A study[4] of the four factors reveals the following principles:

Purpose and Character of the Use: Although *Campbell* said no factor is the key factor, the first factor—the purpose and character of the use—has more weight than the others. It achieves this by neutralizing some of the other factors or affecting how the court will weigh other factors in the balance depending on the purpose and character of the copyist's use.

If the purpose and character of the use is commercial, money-grubbing, and pecuniary in nature, this fact will hurt the score on all of the other factors. Copyright fair use law does not pat people on the back who copy other people's works just to exploit them and make money. If a person is making money from her scheme, she probably can pay for the rights to the work, or so the logic goes. On the other hand, a noncommercial purpose tends to favor fair use, and will help the weighing of other factors on fair use. Again, it is not a guaranty, but it will help to find fairness in the use.

Nature of the Copyrighted Work: Factor two does not turn very many cases from fair to unfair or vice versa, but the factor is weighed in the analysis. Factor two has two main points: the copying of unpublished works, and the degree to which the first work is wholly original and creative. As to the first of these points, if a work is unpublished, keep your hands off of it. Publishing other people's works before they get a chance to is considered unfair. It will rarely qualify as a fair use. Regarding the second point, the courts must consider whether the copyrighted work that was copied is a purely expressive, wholly created work, such as a work of fiction or visual art that is completely original to the author or artist from start to finish. Wholly original and creative works are harder to copy on a fair use basis. But if the work is non-fiction, or contains a significant amount of non-original, non-copyrightable material, it can be copied more readily, subject of course to the other factors.

Amount Taken: With factor three, less is more, meaning the copyist should take as little as she needs, and no more. But the analysis here is heavily dependent on the purpose and character of the use (factor one), and also on the context the copyist is working in, and media involved in the copying. The courts cannot evaluate the amount taken without considering the purpose and character of the use; no predictions can be made on how much is too much without knowing, too much for what purpose?

For example, one of the classic fair uses is parody wherein you copy elements of an earlier work so that you can spoof it and ridicule it. Parody is a form of comment and criticism, and comment and criticism is held to be good First Amendment speech that helps us maintain a robust constitutional democracy. In order to do a proper parody, you have to copy enough of the original work to reveal that which you are ridiculing—and sometimes that requires the copying of a lot of the original material. That is the origin of the word parody—a song sung at the same time as another—and in order to show two works at the same time, the original and the parody, you have do some significant copying. The law accepts these requirements, so if you prove that your purpose and character of use was that of a parody, you will be allowed to copy a lot of the original material.

On the other hand, when the purpose is not parody, copying just a bit too much—more than is minimally needed for your purpose—will get you in the unfair territory on this factor. For example, in educational uses, the amount taken matters a great deal, as does the character of how you use it:

- Simple copying of limited portions for display in class—**sounds fair**

- Copying of entire chapters for use in class—**starts to sound unfair**

- Copying of entire work (articles, books)—**sounds unfair from the get-go**

- Copying an entire work and displaying, publishing, or distributing it further on the web, in course texts, or in college bookstore course packets—**unfair; hire a lawyer now**

Effect on the Market for the Original: The effect on the market for the original work is a somewhat unusual factor. It is of strong lineage, being traced all the way back to Justice Story's 1841 opinion in *Folsom v. Marsh*.[5] Factor four almost always is affected by the purpose and character of the use. A parody or other form of harsh commentary and criticism is likely to have little impact on the market for the original. Fans of the original are unlikely to be interested in things that ridicule the original, and people who are disposed to dislike the original, and thus will pay for the parody, are unlikely to decide to go out and buy the original. Other uses have a one-to-one zero sum effect on the market for the original. Even bona fide public interest-serving uses such as news reporting and education will deprive the owner of a sale if they reprint and give away a copy of the entire original work. In between, you have uses that tend to make the original more popular by bringing attention to the original. If a famous artist copies an obscure work of an obscure artist, the famous artist often will argue that they did the original artist a favor by drawing attention and publicity to the artist. This argument is just that; an argument. Maybe the original owner didn't want that kind of publicity, or didn't want to be associated with the celebrated copyist and his or her activities.

The market effect factor is the most complicated of the factors. It requires the input of economists and accountants to calculate the possible losses from a use. Unless you can slam dunk the fair use at the purpose and character of use stage, you may be in for a long, rough, expensive ride arguing for or against market effect from the use at hand.

In this next section, I will unpack several common fair use situations to illustrate the working of the law, and perhaps to debunk several myths about what can be copied freely and what cannot.

News Reporting

News reporting is a strong First Amendment activity. The press get their own clause in the First Amendment: "Congress shall make no law . . . abridging the freedom of . . . the press." But as with all fair uses, context matters, and the purpose and character of the use matters a great deal.

LA Riot News Footage 1992 Pt.2

During the riots in south central Los Angeles on April 29, 1992, that followed the acquittal of the four white police officers tried for the beating of Rodney King (better look that event up on Google if you don't remember it), Los Angeles News Service captured some remarkable video of rioters pulling a truck driver, Reginald Denny, from his truck and beating him. Los Angeles News Service sends out news helicopters to capture video of news as it is occurring, and they captured some remarkable footage of the riots that day.

The "Reginald Denny Beating" portion of the video in question was 4 minutes and 30 seconds long. Many stations and news services wanted to show the video. Several of them decided not to pay for it, and showed a few key seconds without buying a license and paying a fee. The amount taken was very small, and the purpose and character of the use was news reporting.

Nevertheless, each court that considered the issue held this not to be a fair use. In a series of law suits of Los Angeles News Service against Reuters Television, KCAL-TV, and CBS, each court found that the use failed the four fair use factors.[6] To put these rulings in perspective, it is important to remember that the freedom of the press is another constitutional freedom, believed to be the most important freedom for the preservation of a healthy constitutional democracy. This news footage was current, relevant, up-to-the second information about what was going on in south central Los Angeles. But copyrighted images or footage are not fair game for sampling or other forms of duplication. Even taking very small amounts can be unfair.

You might be wondering why copyright should be able to put a clamp on this news story. The truth is, copyright cannot do it. The idea-expression distinction means that anyone can report on the L.A. riots of April 1992, and on the beating of Reginald Denny. These are facts and ideas, open for anyone to use. What you cannot do is report on the news by stealing LA News Service's footage. You can watch the footage, learn from it, write down what you see, and then make your own expression of what happened. All of that is basic research into the facts that you can harvest to make your own expression of the events. But you cannot copy someone else's creation of a record of what happened and rebroadcast and redistribute that expression without getting permission from the owner and paying for a license.

On the Scene Photographs of Disaster

Reporters and witnesses who are on the scene of major events are likely to capture some of the most highly desired video and visual evidence of the event. When the event is totally and freakishly unexpected, such as an earthquake, terrorist attack, plane crash, or other fast-occurring disaster, the record of the event captured by reporters or witnesses who happen to be at the scene may be unique, and priceless.

A fairly recent instance of this kind of fortuitous presence at the scene of an instantaneous disaster involved the professional photographer, Daniel Morel, who happened to be present in Haiti at the moment a huge earthquake devastated the country in January 2010. Morel left his hotel and took photos of the aftermath of the disaster.[7] He uploaded them to his Twitter-Twitpics account, @photomorel. The photos were striking, and have gone on to win world press awards.

Soon after he posted them, news agencies tried to get in touch with Morel to use some of the pictures, but failed. Then a random third party, Lisandro Suero, retweeted the photos claiming they were his own. Agence France Presse (AFP), during its current events coverage of the quake, grabbed photos from Suero's tweet, and uploaded them to its AFP site. Getty obtained them from AFP, and further lent and licensed them to the Washington Post, and to many news outlets in the world. Morel's photo shown above became *the* cover photo used to illustrate the story of the quake.[8]

Daniel Morel sued Agence France Presse, the Washington Post, and Getty Images for violating his copyrights to the images. All of these news agencies and newspapers raised a fair use right to use Morel's first hand, on the scene, irreplaceable images without authorization and payment. But the defenses were doomed to fail for the same reasons that the claims of the news services who used LA News Service's footage of the beating of Reginald Denny ultimately failed: there is no general fair use for news reporting. News uses must satisfy the same factors as other fair uses.

The law does not weigh heavily the high value of the original to tell the story better than other alternatives—that is a factor that makes the copying *more unfair*, not more fair. If the photo is so stupendous and irreplaceable, then you should pay for it. As with the *LA News Service* footage, you can look at this photo and others, and learn from it, and make your own expression of what happened, even of what you saw in the photograph. What the Morel photo depicts are facts, and you can report the facts—a girl partially covered in rubble, caked in plaster dust, reached out for help minutes after the quake occurred. What you cannot do (for free) is republish and redistribute Morel's expression of those facts that he created through his authorship with a camera.

The Zapruder Film

In the annals of being at the right place at the right (or wrong) time, the name "Abraham Zapruder" will be listed high up on the list. Zapruder's visit to Dealey Plaza in Dallas on November 22, 1963, produced one of the most important works of news and historical footage ever recorded in the form of the short film taken by Zapruder of the assassination of President John F. Kennedy.

Zapruder Frame 312

Life Magazine, who purchased the rights to the film for $150,000 at the time of the events, resisted anyone's unauthorized use of the film for any purpose, news, education, or commentary. Many years later, the U.S. government declared the work to be an assassination record, and took over the copyright to the work. Later still, the rights were donated to the 6th Floor Museum in Dallas at the site of the assassination.

I will discuss one more example that follows nicely on the others.

Fair Use for Political Commentary?

The First Amendment is the patron of fair use in copyright law, and one of the most powerful and protected categories of speech is political speech consisting of commentary on and criticism of elected public figures. In debating the merits of the First Amendment, several of the Founding Fathers agreed that if our American experiment in democratically elected government was to succeed, there must be a free and unrestricted right both to communicate information about candidates and their performance in and qualifications for governing, and to criticize elected leaders. The electorate must be informed about its rulers and their governance, and open and robust commentary and criticism of government must be preserved. The freedom to engage in political speech above all other categories of speech was regarded as the valve on the pressure cooker of public dissent, and it was believed that allowing the steam and heat to be vented through this valve would ultimately foreclose the disaffected from needing to find more violent and destructive ways of communicating their dislike for the government. As a result, political speech became the highest, most cherished form of speech, and its preservation was deemed essential for the health and welfare of a constitutional democracy.

Under the First Amendment, government must have an extraordinarily compelling reason before it can censor political speech. A law censoring political speech receives the highest level of scrutiny, vying only with prior restraints on the press. This law and policy applies to copyright, too, and is further supported by the fact that "comment and criticism" of any kind is deemed to be a classic fair use purpose, recognized in the preamble to section 107 of the code. Use of limited portions of copyrighted materials for illustration of points of comment or criticism is a classic fair use situation. But that is where the free ride ends. The comment and criticism fair use, even in a political speech context, is not a license to reprint the highlights of an original creative work, even if the work has a political message or subject.

The 1985 United States Supreme Court case of *Harper & Row v. Nation Enterprises*[9] drove this point home. In the case, retired President Gerald Ford had contracted with Harper & Row to publish his autobiography, *A Time to Heal*, and Harper made a deal with Time Magazine to print an authorized excerpt of the work in its magazine. Nation Enterprises received a purloined copy of the unpublished manuscript and proceeded to scoop Time and Harper & Row by reprinting verbatim some 300 words of the memoir in *The Nation* magazine.[10]

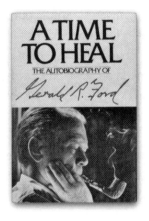

The words were not about Ford's football career at Michigan, or his stellar career in the House of Representatives, nor Ford's take on the several deranged people who tried unsuccessfully to assassinate him. No, the topic of the excerpt was Ford's take on his pardon of disgraced President Nixon, a controversial topic at the time of the pardon, and not much less controversial at the time of the memoirs' excerpted publication in 1979. The excerpt was printed in a magazine known for its political commentary, although the publisher decided to print the excerpt first, and worry about writing commentary about the excerpt later, in its effort to beat the other publishers to press. The excerpt was only a small part of the original memoir which had tens of thousands of words. But the Supreme Court didn't like the fair use claim for two reasons: Reproducing the heart of the work to comment on the work is not fair use. And scooping another publisher by publishing an unpublished excerpt is not an appropriate purpose for a fair use. The fact that it was done in the context of political speech did not change the Court's mind.

Parody—the Granddaddy of Fair Use Exceptions

Parody is an excellent fair use, one of most potent of the classic fair uses. When you have a parody, you are well on your way to a successful fair use analysis. The key is having a **parodic purpose**. A parodic purpose is one to criticize the original work or its author. It will not suffice to criticize society or some other aspect of modern culture—an effort to do this may come in under another exception, but not parody. For a parody, you must show that your purpose is to ridicule the original work or its author. And you must show it in the work itself—it will not suffice for you to write an explanation or give an interview trying to explain that you meant to criticize the work. It must be obvious from the contents of the work itself that there are two songs being sung, the original and your spoof of the original.

If you achieve a purpose and character of parody, the other factors fall neatly into line:

- Parody allows commercial uses of the original material (factor 1);

- You can use famous, extremely valuable, copyrighted works, and produce your parody in the same medium as the original—e.g., a sound recording parody of another sound recording; a motion picture parody of another motion picture (factor 2);

- You get to take vast amounts of the work in order to "conjure up" the original and identify it as the target of your criticism (factor 3); and

- You've got a fair chance to convince the court that your parody will not dilute or undercut the market for the original because people who like and pay for the original are unlikely to want to pay for a spoof of the original (factor 4).

You must convince the court that one of your purposes for creating the work is to make fun of, spoof, or criticize the original work; after that, it will not hurt you that you also wanted to accomplish other objectives with your work. Parody does not have to be the sole purpose or even the primary purpose, as long as *one* purpose for the work was parody.

Parody Example 1

Elsmere Music v. NBC (1980)[11]

Elsmere Music owned the rights to the New York State tourism song, "I love New York," that played incessantly over all broadcast media in the sad times of New York City's financial crisis of 1976-77. This did not escape Saturday Night Live's notice, and the show on NBC staged a spoof comedy sketch featuring a mock Chamber of Commerce meeting for the Biblical city of Sodom that ending with a parodic arrangement of the New York tourism song as "I love Sodom."[12] Prior to the singing of the jingle, the sketch made a series of jokes and innuendo regarding the Biblical town's reputation for gambling, gluttony, idol worshipping, and, of course, sodomy. The jingle that closed the sketch was the only thing that directly connected New York to Sodom.

"I love Sodom" on Saturday Night Live

The trial court wasted little time finding a good, old fashioned parody and satire fair use, following the path paved by *Berlin v. E. C. Publications, Inc.*,[13] which had exonerated certain parody lyrics to Irving Berlin songs printed in Mad Magazine. The court briefly mentioned the 1976 Copyright Act which had just gone into effect at the time of the parody broadcast in May 1977. It held that both "parody and satire are deserving of substantial freedom," and because the "defendants had taken no more of the original song than was necessary to 'recall' or 'conjure up' the object of [the] satire," and as the parody had "neither the intent nor the effect of fulfilling the demand for the original," no infringement had taken place. Thus, the *Elsmere* court equated parody and satire and found that each provided a ground for copyright fair use. The Court of Appeals affirmed the trial court on the basis of the lower court's rationale.

Parody Example 2

Leibovitz v. Paramount Pictures (1998)[14]

The *Leibovitz v. Paramount Pictures* case featured celebrity photographer, Annie Leibovitz and her celebrated cover photo of a hugely pregnant and quite naked Demi Moore on the cover of *Vanity Fair* magazine. At the same time that the *Vanity Fair*-Leibovitz-Moore cover was receiving national attention, Paramount Pictures was in the process of promoting its latest sequel in the *Naked Gun* line of comedic films, and it took the image of Moore from the *Vanity Fair* cover, recreated the shot, and placed *Naked Gun* star Leslie Neilson's head on the pregnant female body.[15]

Leibovitz Cover   Naked Gun 33 1/3 Poster

This case is particularly noteworthy because Paramount created the work in question for an advertisement of a movie, a completely commercial use. Advertisements are referred to in the law as "commercial speech," and if political speech is at the zenith of First Amendment protection, commercial speech is at the nadir. Commercial speech is still speech, but it is the lowest form of protected speech. Nevertheless, Paramount's lawyers argued that the poster was created, in part at least, to criticize Annie Leibovitz and to spoof the way she created the Moore cover photo. Apparently, the court could find this meaning and purpose just by looking at the two works. In any event, the court agreed with this theory and found a parody fair use. Leibovitz's artistic approach was deemed to be pretentious, using a classical "Modest Venus" pose from Botticelli's Venus, and approaching the work with a serious artistic flair, even though Moore was a more of a pop film star than glamour icon, and her pregnancy was less of an artistic event and more suited for check-out line tabloid material than mythology. Paramount was allowed to take a large portion of the work in order to turn it on its head, and prevailed on its parody fair use defense.

Contemporary Transformative Fair Uses[16]

The list of public purposes for fair use is not exclusive, and in the area of visual arts, it has been expanded in recent years by the overarching, non-codified, but massively important concept of **transformation**. Transformation is now the X-factor, the factor not listed in section 107, the one factor that can make or break certain expressive uses of works. Highly transformed works are fair; non-transformed works must find some other justification for their fairness (such as a classic fair use for education or comment and criticism).

The formula that led the Supreme Court to adopt the overarching fair use concept of transformation is deceptively simple: Transformation of existing material creates new material—new expression that communicates new ideas and new meaning through new content or a new context. And the promotion of new expression to benefit the public was the reason we have copyright protection in the first place.

The transformative test looks to whether a fair use merely supersedes the objects and intentions of the original work—meaning, does it simply take the whole or part of the original and repeat it for its original expressive purpose—or does the new work add something new, creating new content, meaning and expression, because of some transformative treatment of the original material. The transformation can be by adding an overwhelming amount of new content, so that the original work no longer shines through in the final work. It can also be by "recontextualizing" the original work—placing it in a new context so that it no longer serves the same function and purpose for which it originally was created. The new function and purpose should be something beneficial to the public (although it usually benefits the new user, too).

The problem is that transformation, and its companion words, transform, transformative, and transformativeness, are a family of concepts that are difficult to define and even more difficult to use to predict whether certain uses are transformative or not. The analysis of this issue begins with the case that started the transformative craze, *Campbell v. Acuff Rose Music*.[17]

Updated Lyrics Become a Transformative Parody

Campbell v. Acuff Rose Music (1994)

This chapter has cited the *Campbell v. Acuff Rose Music* case several times, but I have not discussed the facts of the case. Campbell involves a recording by The 2Live Crew rap group on its *As Nasty as They Wanna Be* album that purports to parody and ridicule a famous pop ballad by Roy Orbison, *Pretty Woman*. The case is particularly noteworthy for fair use purposes because in it the Supreme Court adopted the transformative test for copyright fair use law.

The Supreme Court did not write the transformative test—it was taken from a law review article written by Judge Pierre Leval[18]—but the Supreme Court incorporated the test into the fair use analysis. The result was a new factor, one that ties together much of the policy that has supported the interpretation and application of the other factors.

In the *Campbell* case, the lyrics provide the narrative of parody and ridicule of the original work:

"Oh, Pretty Woman" by Roy Orbison and William Dees

Pretty Woman, walking down the street,

Pretty Woman, the kind I like to meet,

Pretty Woman, I don't believe you, you're not the truth,

No one could look as good as you

Mercy

Pretty Woman, won't you pardon me,

Pretty Woman, I couldn't help but see,

Pretty Woman, that you look lovely as can be

Are you lonely just like me?

Pretty Woman, stop a while,

Pretty Woman, talk a while,

Pretty Woman give your smile to me

Pretty Woman, yeah, yeah, yeah

Pretty Woman, look my way,

Pretty Woman, say you'll stay with me

'Cause I need you, I'll treat you right

Come to me baby, Be mine tonight

Pretty Woman, don't walk on by,

Pretty Woman, don't make me cry,

Pretty Woman, don't walk away,

Hey, O.K.

If that's the way it must be, O.K.

I guess I'll go on home, it's late

There'll be tomorrow night, but wait!

What do I see

Is she walking back to me?

Yeah, she's walking back to me!

Oh, Pretty Woman.

"Pretty Woman" as recorded by 2 Live Crew

Pretty woman walkin' down the street

Pretty woman girl you look so sweet

Pretty woman you bring me down to that knee

Pretty woman you make me wanna beg please

Oh, pretty woman

Big hairy woman you need to shave that stuff

Big hairy woman you know I bet it's tough

Big hairy woman all that hair it ain't legit

'Cause you look like 'Cousin It'

Big hairy woman

Bald headed woman girl your hair won't grow

Bald headed woman you got a teeny weeny afro

Bald headed woman you know your hair could look nice

Bald headed woman first you got to roll it with rice

Bald headed woman here, let me get this hunk of biz for ya

Ya know what I'm saying you look better than rice a roni

Oh bald headed woman

Big hairy woman come on in

And don't forget your bald headed friend

Hey pretty woman let the boys Jump in

Two timin' woman girl you know you ain't right

Two timin' woman you's out with my boy last night

Two timin' woman that takes a load off my mind

Two timin' woman now I know the baby ain't mine

Oh, two timin' woman

Oh pretty woman.

The court found that the changes to the lyrics identified the naiveté of the original Roy Orbison ballad and spoofed it for its sentimental crooning about a romance with a streetwalker (although, Roy Orbison probably just meant an attractive woman walking down the street, not a prostitute). The two works are available for your listening and review on the internet: https://www.youtube.com/watch?v=ssXAkgObV6o (original); https://www.youtube.com/watch?v=65GQ70Rf_8Y (2 Live Crew parody).

The 2 Live Crew recording came out in 1989, and ironically, the motion picture, *Pretty Woman,* came out several months later in 1990. *Pretty Woman* the movie was about a man who falls in love with a streetwalker of the prostitute variety, but in a romantic, sentimental plot twist, the two wind up together for happily ever after, thus fulfilling Orbison's sentiments (Orbison's work also was used in the film's soundtrack) much more than 2 Live Crew's scorn (the 2 Live Crew version was not used). In any event, the Supreme Court found 2 Live Crew's version to be a highly transformative use of the Orbison song, and found it to be a fair use.

Transformation Without Parody—A Successful Satire

Blanch v. Koons (2006)[19]

As copyright fair use case law turned the corner from the 1990's to the early 2000's, the breadth of the transformative fair use protection began slowly to expand. A line of cases in the United States Courts of Appeals for the Second Circuit and Ninth Circuit added several narratives to the list of successful transformative fair uses.[20] One area of fair use that was rescued from the "unfair use" list was satires.

Satires had had a good run in fair use jurisprudence up to the *Campbell* case. As noted in the example of *Elsmere Music v. NBC*[21] discussed above, the Saturday Night Live TV show that spoofed the New York State tourism song, "I Love New York," and made it into "I Love Sodom," was equal parts satire as it was parody, and the court described it so. But the *Campbell* case in 1994 put the kibosh on satires for over a decade.

The *Campbell* case compared parodies to satires, and held that parodies use another person's material to make fun of that material or the person who created it, while satire just uses another person's material in a general spoof of modern life or as a vehicle to criticize something or someone specific, but not the original author or the original material. The important distinction the Supreme Court focused on was that satire does not make an obvious attempt to criticize the earlier material it borrows; more often it chooses the material because it is useful in making the satirist's point without any criticism of the original material or its author. Parodists need to borrow large portions of an earlier work so as to identify for the audience the subject of the parody's attack. Satirists just choose the earlier material because it is useful, or fun, and it suits the satirist's needs. The Supreme Court endorsed parodies as a transformative fair use, but stated that satires needed additional justification for their use of someone else's work.

This treatment held back the satire world for quite some time, at least in terms of cases that made their way through the courts. The *Dr. Seuss* case[22] was a casualty of this thinking. The case involved a comic portrayal of the famous and highly publicized O.J. Simpson murder trial in a book entitled *The Cat Not in the Hat* that borrowed the artistic style and rhyming scheme of the Dr. Seuss book, *The Cat in the Hat*. The new work used the art and poetic style of the iconic Dr. Seuss work for a completely new function and purpose, and the authors made drastic alterations to the content of the book. Nevertheless, the court wound up categorizing the work as a satire, not a parody, because the new work did not appear to criticize anything about Dr. Seuss himself or *The Cat in the Hat*. Since parodies were fair, and satires were unfair, the court denied the defendants' fair use defense.

Eventually, a famous artist named Jeffrey Koons took a case all the way to the United States Court of Appeals for the Second Circuit, and argued that his satire of fashion and society's tastes should count as a transformative fair use. Koons took the work of a photographer named Blanch. Blanch's work, *Silk Sandals,* was standard fare fashion photography—a shapely set of sandals on a shapely woman's feet. The Koons work, *Niagara,* recontextualized the image into a splashy scene of four women's legs and feet hanging down somewhat like Niagara Falls (which itself appears in the background), in the context of fatty and sugary foods. Koon's asserted that the work commented on society's tastes and motivations regarding food and women's fashions. It was clear that the work was not a criticism of Blanch or her photography. He used her work solely because it was one indicative example of how women are photographed in fashion advertising. Koons dressed up the basic fashion photography through painting.[23]

Blanch's Silk Sandals   Koons' Niagara

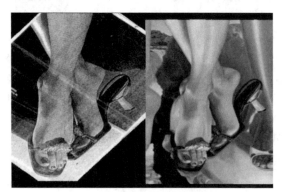

Nevertheless, the court liked it. The court thought Koons had a genuine creative rationale for borrowing Blanch's image, rather than using it merely to get attention or avoid the drudgery of working up something fresh. In other words, the predominant purpose for his use of the work was creative and expressive, not commercial and exploitive, and the recontextualization and massive alteration in content created a new work with new content, meaning, and expression that was very different in purpose and function from Blanch's original work. All of this added up to a transformative fair use, albeit a satire, not a parody.

Applying Your Own Bold Style as Transformation

Cariou v. Prince (2013)[24]

Richard Prince is an unabashed, unapologetic appropriationist artist. In 2007 and 2008, Prince appropriated photographs of Rastafarians in their native environment that had been taken by photographer, Patrick Cariou, and compiled in Cariou's book, *Yes Rasta*. As described in the appellate opinion,

> Prince had a show at the Eden Rock hotel in St. Barth's that included a collage, titled *Canal Zone* (2007), comprising 35 photographs torn out of *Yes Rasta* and pinned to a piece of plywood. Prince altered those photographs significantly, by among other things painting "lozenges" over their subjects' facial features and using only portions of some of the images. In June 2008, Prince purchased three additional copies of *Yes Rasta*. He went on to create thirty additional artworks in the Canal Zone series, twenty-nine of which incorporated partial or whole images from *Yes Rasta*. The portions of Yes Rasta photographs used, and the amount of each artwork that they constitute, vary significantly from piece to piece.[25]

A sampling of the Canal Zone images are shown below:[26]

The trial court granted summary judgment in favor of Cariou finding that Prince's images were not transformative and Prince had not established a fair use defense regarding the images.[27] The Second Circuit reversed, in part because it believed the District Court had interpreted and applied the transformative test incorrectly, relying too much on the concept that a transformative work must "comment on, relate to the historical context of, or critically refer back to the original works."[28] The Second Circuit interpreted the law differently:

> The law imposes no requirement that a work comment on the original or its author in order to be considered transformative, and a secondary work may constitute a fair use even if it serves some purpose other than those (criticism, comment, news reporting, teaching, scholarship, and research) identified in the preamble to the statute. [Campbell, 510 U.S.] at 577, 114 S.Ct. 1164; Harper & Row, 471 U.S. at 561, 105 S.Ct. 2218. Instead, as the Supreme Court as well as decisions from our court have emphasized, to qualify as a fair use, a new work

generally must alter the original with "new expression, meaning, or message." Campbell, 510 U.S. at 579, 114 S.Ct. 1164; see also Blanch, 467 F.3d at 253 (original must be employed "in the creation of new information, new aesthetics, new insights and understandings" (quotation marks omitted)); Castle Rock, 150 F.3d at 142.

The court was impressed with the additions Prince made to Cariou's *Yes Rasta* works, the lozenges imposed over facial features and childlike line drawings on the photos, and found that Prince had scored highly on the first fair use factor, "the purpose and character of the use," by his transformative treatments, and also on the fourth fair use factor, "the effect on the market for the original," because his works served a completely different, "high end" art market that did not usurp Cariou's own market.[29] Prince also scored well enough on the second and third factors to preserve his fair use defense.[30] The Second Circuit reversed the District Court's ruling and ordered summary judgment in favor of Prince on all but five of his thirty works in the *Canal Zone* show, choosing to remand these five to the District Court for further consideration.[31] These five had fewer and more minimal alterations than the other works from the Canal Zone show. Two of the five works are shown here—Cariou's photograph appears on the left of each grouping, Prince's work on the right:

After remand, the lawsuit settled.[32]

A Green Light for Transformation

Seltzer v. Green Day (2013)[33]

Street artist, Dereck Seltzer, is the creator of a street artwork entitled, *Scream Icon* (shown below). Seltzer sued the alternative/punk rock group Green Day and Roger Staub, an artist who created the backgrounds for Green Day videos, because Staub used a modified version of *Scream Icon* (an unauthorized derivative work) as a prominent part of a backdrop of graffiti art that served as the background design for the music video and concert staging of a specific song, East Jesus Nowhere, http://www.youtube.com/watch?v=iPu18Wt8e7Y. The modifications to *Scream Icon* were a large red cross and several markings and scratches superimposed on the face of the image. As revealed in the video, much of which contains concert footage, the modified *Scream Icon* image was placed roughly at center stage behind the rock group, and it was larger than the other images placed on either side of it.

Scream Icon[34]

Modified Scream Icon as Displayed in the Concert Footage and Music Video of Green Day's East Jesus Nowhere. [35]

The District Court and the Ninth Circuit both found the *Scream Icon* work had been transformed both by the artistic overlay of the red cross and other markings, and by the recontextualization of the work with other works in the concert presentation of a specific song whose theme is "the hypocrisy of some religious people who preach one thing but act otherwise . . . [and] the violence that is done in the name of religion."[36] The Ninth Circuit went back to basics, quoting the grandfather of the transformative test, Pierre Laval:

> The use must be productive and must employ the quoted matter in a different manner or for a different purpose from the original. A quotation of copyrighted material that merely repackages or republishes the original is unlikely to pass the test; in Justice Story's words, it would merely "supersede the objects" of the original. If, on the other hand, the secondary use adds value to the original— if the quoted matter is used as raw material, transformed in the creation of new information, new aesthetics, new insights and understandings—this is the very type of activity that the fair use doctrine intends to protect for the enrichment of society.[37]

The court found the band and its artistic designer prevailed on each factor of the fair use test in 17 U.S.C. § 107.[38] This is a noteworthy holding, because the context of the use of the *Scream Icon* was a commercial, for-profit enterprise, and in particular, a music video intended to advertise and promote the music sales and concert ticket sales of the rock band, yet the physical changes and recontextualization of the *Scream Icon* work from street art to concert stage-dress was deemed to be a transformative fair use.

Lessons on How to Be "Transformative"[39]

The lessons to be learned from the precedents are the following: "Transformation" is best achieved with a change in the purpose and character of the original work. It is evident from the record of cases above that the courts take the "purpose" part of that rule very seriously, for all of the approved fair uses in the appellate cases involved a change in the predominant purpose for the use of the work rather than simply a change in the character (the form, the contents) of the work. Even if the works were not changed in form, function, or genre, the fair use works were transformed in predominant purpose either through alteration of the contents, or recontextualization of the copied material, or by the addition of significant creative expression so that the predominant purpose of the new work was significantly different from the original work. Non-alteration of the contents and expression of artistic and literary works still can be justified as fair use, but the function and purpose of the original works must be changed in the second works in a manner that fulfills fair use objectives that promote the progress of the arts and the creation of new, original expression that benefits the public.

The strongest transformative fair uses are those that modify the contents, function, and purpose in a significant and obvious manner, turning the meaning of the original work on its head, or openly criticizing the original work. Uses that do not modify the contents, function, or purpose of the original works in a significant and obvious manner fail the transformative test and are found not to be fair.

The most troubling fair use cases for secondary users of artistic or literary works are those, such as *Dr. Seuss*, that appear to have greatly altered significant aspects of the original works, but were not found to be fair uses. These seemingly incongruous outcomes may be explained by looking to the common underpinning and public policy objectives pursued by the courts in these opinions: even significant alteration of the form, or genre, or theme, or tone, or even the overall meaning of the works will not be found to be fair use if some of the creative, artistic, and expressive virtues of the original works are not replaced or overwhelmed by the expression in the second work. If the creative, artistic, and expressive virtues of the original works still are discernible in the second work and still add value to the secondary work, the use of the original work will be deemed unfair.

The transformative test has changed copyright law, and it has become the defining standard for fair use. Copyright law seeks first to promote new, original expression in the arts and literature, and second to allow other public interest activities such as education, research, archiving, news reporting, and comment and criticism of existing works. Transformation requires the copier to fulfill these objectives. The duplication of works just to show off their same creative, artistic, or literary virtues in a new time, a new place, a new mode or medium of communication, or for a new audience does not fulfill the goals of copyright. No new and original expression results from simple replication of the same communication and expression found in the original. The derivative works doctrine gives those rights to the original author or artist, not to the public at large.

The lessons of the transformative test for those engaged in creative, artistic, or literary pursuits may be summed up in the following: if you copy an original work, use it for a different purpose than the purpose for which the original work was created. Modify the contents, function, and meaning of the original work through alteration of the original expression or the addition of significant new expression. Otherwise, you are making an unauthorized exploitation of the creative expression of the work for exactly the same reasons and purposes that the original author or artist created the work, and you are depriving the original author or artist of the derivative works right guaranteed by copyright.

Review and Discussion—Fair or Unfair Uses

Which of the following new works are likely to be found to be fair uses? Consider transformation by recontextualization as well as by changing the content. Are any of these obvious parodies? Remember that parodies have to be obvious just by looking at the two works. Have any of these works changed the function and purpose of the original works in a way that should lead to a finding of transformation and fair use?

	Original Work	New Work
9.1		
	Mickey Mouse as a pilot of a mail plane, delivering mail bags through thick and thin	Mickey Mouse and other Disney characters running drugs (i.e., bags of "dope") in counter-cultural comic
9.2		
	Tongue in cheek Sci Fi comedy film where government agents battle alien life on earth—"Protecting the earth from the scum of the universe"	Mockumentary where Michael Moore takes on big industry to ridicule its greed and arrogance—"Protecting the earth from the scum of corporate America"

9.3

Barney Google and Spark
Plug cartoon

Three-dimensional trinkets
based on Barney Google and
Spark Plug cartoon

(See Discussion and Answers on the page that follows.)

Discussion and Answers—Fair or Unfair Uses

9.1 Walt Disney vs. Air Pirates	This was an actual litigation,[40] but one that predated *Campbell*. Under current law, it appears difficult for the second work, *Air Pirates*, to claim a fair use of the original Disney creation, *Mickey Mouse the Mail Pilot*. We only have the cover art to look at, but *Air Pirates* has taken the entire image, only switching out bags of mail for bags of "dope" tied to the tail of the plane. There is not a great deal of commentary and criticism evidenced by this use, and not a great deal of transformation. The contents of the *Air Pirates* works would have added more to the analysis because *Air Pirates* did present a whole new take on the Disney world, with Disney characters in counter-cultural situations of drug use and promiscuity. But for this example, no fair use is evident. (This also was the rule in the lawsuit that predated *Campbell*).
9.2 Columbia Pictures (*Men in Black*) vs. Miramax Films Corp. (*The Big One*)	*Men in Black* and *The Big One*. The overlapping features of the two works are the unusually big, shiny guns matched against an unusually big, shiny microphone; the black suits and black shades paired with a black suit and black shades; and the characters posed in oversized perspective against a New York skyline at nightfall on both covers. Is *The Big One* spoofing *Men in Black*? That would be hard to do, because *Men in Black* already is over-the-top silly and funny. It would be better to pick a straight target for your parody (Annie

	Leibovitz and her deadly serious approach to her photography, for example), not a silly, humorous target. There is little else to claim as transformation. Most likely Miramax would not have a fair use (which was the ruling in the actual litigation).[41]
9.3 Barney Google and Sparkplug vs. 3-D trinkets	The derivative works right precludes the creation of 3-D derivative works based on 2-D cartoons. The trinkets would constitute an infringement of the cartoon creations.[42]

---

[1] The Statute of Anne, also known as the Copyright Act 1710, 8 Ann. c. 19, 21.

[2] *Folsom v. Marsh*, 9. F. Cas. 342 (C.C.D. Mass. 1841) (Story, J.), is widely regarded as the first "fair use" case in American copyright jurisprudence.

[3] *Campbell v. Acuff-Rose Music*, 510 U.S. 569 (1994).

[4] This section draws heavily from my study and synthesis of the application of the section 107 fair use factors in United States Courts of Appeals' decisions after *Campbell*. *See* Michael D. Murray, *What is Transformative? An Explanatory Synthesis of the Convergence of Transformation and Predominant Purpose in Copyright Fair Use Law*, 11 CHIC.-KENT J. INTELL. PROP. 260 (2012).

[5] *Folsom*, 9. F. Cas. 342 (fair use analysis considers whether the second use "supersedes the object[ives]" for the creation of the original).

[6] *Los Angeles News Serv. v. CBS Broad., Inc.*, 305 F.3d 924, 929 (9th Cir.), *opinion amended and superseded*, 313 F.3d 1093 (9th Cir. 2002); *Los Angeles News Serv. v. Reuters Television Int'l, Ltd.*, 149 F.3d 987, 993 (9th Cir. 1998), *as amended on denial of reh'g and reh'g en banc* (Aug. 25, 1998); *Los Angeles News Serv. v. KCAL-TV Channel 9*, 108 F.3d 1119, 1120 (9th Cir. 1997).

[7] Image: Michael D. Murray, Thumbnail-Sized Excerpt of Daniel Morel's Photograph of Haiti Earthquake Victim (2014).

[8] Michael D. Murray, Collage of Thumbnail Excerpts of Newspaper Covers Depicting Daniel Morel's Photograph of Haiti Earthquake Victim (2014).

[9] *Harper & Row Publishers, Inc. v. Nation Enters.*, 471 U.S. 539 (1985).

[10] Images: Michael D. Murray, Thumbnail-Sized Excerpts of Cover of Gerald Ford's Biography, *A Time to Heal*; and Thumbnail-Sized Excerpt of Cover of Nation Magazine's Article Excerpting Gerald Ford's Biography, *A Time to Heal*, the subject matter of *Harper & Row Publishers, Inc. v. Nation Enters.*, 471 U.S. 539 (1985).

[11] *Elsmere Music, Inc. v. National Broadcasting Co.*, 482 F. Supp. 741, 747 (S.D.N.Y. 1980).

[12]   Image: Michael D. Murray, Thumbnail-Sized Excerpt of a Single Frame from Saturday Night Live Skit "I Love Sodom".

[13]   *Berlin v. E. C. Publications, Inc.*, 329 F.2d 541, 543 (2d Cir. 1964).

[14]   *Leibovitz v. Paramount Pictures Corp.*, 137 F.3d 109, 110 (2d Cir. 1998).

[15]   Images: Michael D. Murray, Thumbnail-Sized Excerpt of Vanity Fair Cover Depicting Annie Leibovitz Photograph of Demi Moore; and thumbnail-Sized Excerpt of Naked Gun 33 1/3 Movie Poster Depicting Leslie Neilson in a Pose Reminiscent of Demi Moore on Vanity Fair at Issue in *Leibovitz v. Paramount Pictures Corp.*, 137 F.3d 109, 110 (2d Cir. 1998).

[16]   This section again draws heavily from my study and synthesis of the application of the section 107 fair use factors in United States Courts of Appeals' decisions after *Campbell*. *See* Michael D. Murray, *What is Transformative? An Explanatory Synthesis of the Convergence of Transformation and Predominant Purpose in Copyright Fair Use Law*, 11 Chic.-Kent J. Intell. Prop. 260 (2012).

[17]   *Campbell v. Acuff-Rose Music*, 510 U.S. 569 (1994).

[18]   Pierre N. Leval, *Toward a Fair Use Standard*, 103 Harv. L. Rev. 1105 (1990).

[19]   *Blanch v. Koons*, 467 F.3d 244, 252 (2d Cir. 2006).

[20]   *Leibovitz v. Paramount Pictures Corp.*, 137 F.3d 109, 110 (2d Cir. 1998); *Suntrust Bank v. Houghton Mifflin Co.*, 268 F.3d 1257 (11th Cir. 2001); *Mattel Inc. v. Walking Mountain Prods.*, 353 F.3d 792 (9th Cir. 2003); *Blanch v. Koons*, 467 F.3d 244, 252 (2d Cir. 2006); *Bill Graham Archives v. Dorling Kindersley Ltd.*, 448 F.3d 605, 608-09 (2d Cir. 2006); *Perfect 10, Inc. v. Amazon.com, Inc.*, 508 F.3d 1146 (9th Cir. 2007).

[21]   *Elsmere Music, Inc. v. National Broadcasting Co.*, 482 F. Supp. 741 (S.D.N.Y. 1980).

[22]   *Dr. Seuss Ents., LP v. Penguin Books USA*, 109 F.3d 1394 (9th Cir. 1997).

[23]   Images: Michael D. Murray, Collage of Thumbnail Images Including Excerpt from Blanch's Silk Sandals, Excerpt from Koon's Niagara, Grayscale Comparison of Blanch's Feet to Koon's Treatment of the Feet, all of which relate to the subject matter of *Blanch v. Koons*, 467 F.3d 244 (2d Cir. 2006).

[24]   *Cariou v. Prince*, 714 F.3d 694 (2d Cir.), *cert. denied*, 134 S. Ct. 618 (2013).

[25]   *Cariou*, 714 F.3d at 699-700 (inner footnote omitted).

[26]   Images: Michael D. Murray, Collage of Thumbnail Images of Prince's Canal Zone Works at Issue in the Lawsuit *Cariou v. Prince*, 714 F.3d 694, 699-700 (2d Cir. 2013).

[27]   *Cariou v. Prince*, 784 F. Supp. 2d 337, 349-50 (S.D.N.Y. 2011).

[28]   *Cariou*, 714 F.3d at 706 (referring to *Cariou*, 784 F. Supp. 2d at 348).

[29]   *Id.* at 708-10.

[30]   *Id.*

[31]   *Id.* at 710.

[32]   David McAfee, *Artist Prince, Photographer Cariou Settle Fair Use Feud* (March 18, 2014, 9:27 PM ET), http://www.law360.com/articles/519819/artist-prince-photographer-cariou-settle-fair-use-feud.

[33]   *Seltzer v. Green Day, Inc.*, 725 F.3d 1170, 1175-79 (9th Cir. 2013).

[34]   Images: Michael D. Murray, Thumbnail-Sized Excerpt of Seltzer's *Scream Icon* (2015).

[35]   Images: Michael D. Murray, Thumbnail-Sized Excerpt of One Frame from Concert Footage from the Music Video for Green Day's *East Jesus Nowhere* (2015).

[36]   *Seltzer*, 725 F.3d at 1174.

[37] *Id.* at 1176 (quoting Leval, *Toward a Fair Use Standard*, 103 HARV. L. REV. at 1111).

[38] *Id.* at 1175-79.

[39] Once again, the recommendations of this section draw heavily from my study and synthesis of the application of the section 107 fair use factors in United States Courts of Appeals' decisions after *Campbell*. *See* Michael D. Murray, *What is Transformative? An Explanatory Synthesis of the Convergence of Transformation and Predominant Purpose in Copyright Fair Use Law*, 11 CHIC.-KENT J. INTELL. PROP. 260 (2012).

[40] *Walt Disney Prods. v. Air Pirates*, 581 F.2d 751 (9th Cir. 1978), *cert. denied*, 439 U.S. 1132 (1979).

[41] *Columbia Pictures v. Miramax Films*, 11 F. Supp. 2d 1179 (C.D. Cal. 1998).

[42] *See King Features Syndicate v. Fleischer*, 299 F. 533, 535-37 (2d Cir. 1924).

CHAPTER 10

Steps of a Copyright Dispute

Copyright litigation follows a distinctive path through the points of analysis laid out in the chapters above. This chapter[1] will discuss the steps of a copyright dispute in order to review the issues and considerations of copyright that we have analyzed throughout this book, and it will show how they fit into the context of an actual dispute. The insights revealed here will be useful to lawyers and law students in forming strategies for each stage of the dispute. For all readers, this section will reinforce the rules and concepts we have been examining above, and add to these some additional material that factors into the evaluation of whether the facts and circumstances of a dispute over similar works will sustain a copyright claim for infringement.

Step One: Determine the Act of Copying

The theme and purpose of the dispute will center on an act of copying. I mentioned in Chapter 1 that an act of copying is very important to a copyright case. Copyright protection prevents direct or derivative acts that copy the elements of an original creative work. Therefore, our starting point for the discussion is a dispute over material that appears to have been copied. At step one, no litigation has been filed or even threatened, because the steps require the analysis of several factors that will determine if litigation is warranted or advisable.

At this point in the process, the two parties to the dispute shall be called the copyright owner and the copyist. To be fair, we should call the first party the alleged copyright owner and the second party the alleged copyist. The owner may wind up in the analysis holding an empty bag instead of a copyright; the doctrines of originality, idea-expression, merger, scènes à faire, and functionality may strip the so-called work down to a nub of uncopyrightable nothingness. And the copyist is only thought to be a copyist at the initial stage. Later, after we establish that this party is a true copyist, we might assign other terms to this party—infringer, defendant, or fair user.

Step Two: Register the Copyright if Needed

The dispute can go no further than a war of words, demands, and proposals for settlement unless **registration** of the copyright with the Register of Copyrights in the Library of Congress occurs. This step is required before a lawsuit can be filed. As discussed in Chapter 1, copyright suits can only be brought in federal court, and federal courts require the copyright to be registered.

You can police your work and make demands and proposals concerning it whenever you see someone else copying the work even before you register your copyright to the work. The step of registering the copyright is simply a necessary step that will allow you to file a lawsuit if this step turns out to be necessary. However, the advantage of registering earlier than that point is that you can receive fairly generous statutorily appointed damages for each act of infringement after federal registration, which saves the time and effort of proving your actual damages in the lawsuit (which *is* a significant benefit, as discussed further in Chapter 1).

Step Three: Determine if You Have a Viable Copyright

Step three is necessary because the time to confirm or reconfirm that you or your client possesses a valid and viable copyright is before you make a demand or file a lawsuit. A viable copyright has protectable elements that allegedly have been copied. Throughout the book, I have pointed out the factors and doctrines that can rebut the notion that you or your client actually holds a valid, enforceable copyright with protectable elements that may have been copied, namely the expression and fixation requirements (Chapter 1), the originality and creativity requirements (Chapter 2), the idea-expression distinction (Chapter 3), the scènes à faire and merger doctrines (Chapter 4), and the useful articles doctrine (Chapter 5).

The work needs to be **expressive** and **fixed in a tangible medium**. Expression is a very broad concept—almost anything that is perceivable by the senses communicates something, even if it is a shallow and basic concept such as a color, shape, hardness, weight, smell, or sound (although these shallow and basic concepts most likely will fail the test under the originality and creativity requirements we will get to in a moment).

Expression most likely will not a problem for your copyright analysis, but your claim might end at this step of the analysis if the expression is not **fixed**. The expression might be ephemeral or fleeting, such as a conversation in an elevator, a speech delivered without a script, an impromptu session of choreography performed at a night club, or a jazz improv session performed without music, annotations, and without simultaneous recording. All of these fleeting expressions are uncopyrightable until they are fixed. So, if you are reading this advice before you find yourself in an actual dispute, get out the camera, get out the tape recorder, get out the video camera and record that dance move, tape that improv session, or photograph that drawing in the sand before the tide washes it away forever.

Next we consider the **originality** of the owner's expression. Not every part of the work needs to be original, but in particular, the material or elements of the work that are believed to have been copied must be examined to determine whether these portions originate with the author. However easy it is to state the topic of this inquiry, the actual analysis is fairly loaded with questions, because the concept of "originality" runs to several other concepts and doctrines of this area.

As noted in the initial chapters cited above, the basic idea of originality is that the copied portions of the work originate with the author, and that they are therefore not copied. Scènes à faire in visual art refers to images we call stock images that the author copied or at least adapted for her own expressions. Merged ideas and expression are not original to one artist. Some arrangements and compilations of uncopyrightable material are held to be original, providing new expression that is attributable to the artist; others are held to be so unimaginative and predictable (alphabetical order of list items, numeric order of numbers, etc.) that they are held not to be material originating with the author.

Creativity is a separate requirement, made all the more troublesome because it sounds like a redundant synonym for originality. However, neither originality nor creativity require cleverness, innovation, freshness, or uniqueness. Instead, creativity is a requirement that demands that the work must first be conceived in the mind of the author, then executed into expression that is fixed in a tangible medium. This again is not as simple as it may seem—there are many instances where the problem concerns the use of preexisting material that was taken and worked into the work, not conceived of and executed as the work. Things that are taken and not created are not part of the author's copyright. This side of creativity also drives the other doctrines we have mentioned, merger, scènes à faire, and a chunk of the idea-expression distinction.

The **idea-expression distinction** prevents the copyrighting of ideas. This is a simple concept to state, but it leads to the exclusion of all concepts, techniques, processes, procedures, methods, formulae, and recipes. It also circles back to provide the foundation for much of the merger and scènes à faire doctrines in the area of ideas merged with their expression, and images that are deemed to be essential to the communication of an idea. The actual outward appearance of things—animals, objects, people—fills in the remainder of the scènes à faire doctrine.

Under the **useful articles doctrine**, a practical analysis will test the **functionality** and **utility** of the owner's copyrighted material. If the work has utility, the court will look to see if there are creative, expressive parts that are physically separable (such as the statuette bases for the lamps in *Mazer*), or elements of decoration or ornamentation that are conceptually separable from the functioning of the work (such as the ornamental stone carving around the top of a baptismal font). Under current law (discussed in Chapter 5 above), "separable" means that the allegedly copyrightable parts of the item must be able to be seen or imagined as a separate copyrightable work of pictorial or sculptural art. If the allegedly copyrightable parts of the work cannot be separated from the useful functions of the work physically or by one's imagination, then these parts of the work are not copyrightable.

All of these tests—originality, idea-expression, merger, scènes à faire, and functionality-utility—are a stress on the owner's copyright that might turn a properly thick copyright, with a broad scope of protection against duplicates and unauthorized derivative works, into a thin copyright. A **thin copyright** prevents little else than nearly exact duplication of the work. The court might find the plaintiff's copyright to be so thin that it cannot possibly preclude the defendant's work, and it will dismiss the law suit.

Step Four: Gather the Evidence That the Work Has Been Copied

Here, I am not repeating step one or step three above, but instead I am moving on to examine the proof of the act of copying itself. We previously discussed the need for copying in step 1 of this chapter and in Chapter 1 of this book. Copyright prevents copying, not independent creation, so copying is a requirement of the suit that the plaintiff must establish. One easy way to prove copying is to catch the culprit in the act of copying. That is pretty rare, but some copyists are so comfortable with their life of intellectual piracy that they leave a very good paper trail that establishes the act of duplication.

A second easy way to prove copying is for the copyist to admit he copied. That might happen from time to time, especially where the copyist believes he has a strong fair use defense; it will sound more logical to admit the copying rather than deny it and then say "but I have an excuse."

In all other cases, the copyright owner must prove access to the work plus substantial similarity. As discussed in Chapter 1, there are multiple ways to attempt to prove defendant's access to the work:

- Publication of the work in magazines that defendant subscribes to;
- Publication of the work on the internet, and proof that defendant had internet access;
- Showing of the work at a gallery exhibition, and proof that defendant attended that exhibition;

- Proof of distribution to the defendant, such as where defendant was a judge of an art fair or contest where the work was submitted for consideration, or the defendant was a professor or instructor and the work was submitted to the defendant as classwork.

- If evidence of actual access or probable access is fairly thin, there is one saving grace that might apply: **Striking similarity.** If the two works in question look like nearly exact duplicates—with remarkable, extreme, striking, nearly exact, or breathtaking similarity—then the court may be persuaded that the defendant somehow must have had access to the work because it stretches the imagination to consider that random independent creation with that degree of similarity is possible.

Review of the Interaction of Factors Regarding Access

Q. Do you need to prove access if you have evidence of actual copying?

A. No. Evidence of actual copying obviates need for traditional proof of access.

Q. What if the two works are very similar—do you still need proof of access?

A. Extreme similarity (striking similarity, near identity, virtually identical) of two works may overcome limited evidence of access.

The evidence must establish that there is substantial similarity as to the ***protected elements*** of the work. Therefore, the proof of access must indicate that these protected elements were part of the work that the defendant had access to. For example, if you are attempting to prove that the copyist created an unauthorized derivative of a screenplay, but your proof of access is that the copyist only had access to an early draft of the screenplay, and not the final, you may have problems proving the necessary access. It matters not if unprotected elements of the work are copied or adapted in a derivative work; non-original material, scènes à faire material, processes or procedures, or functional parts of the first work can be copied without copyright implications.

At this stage, **substantial similarity** is evaluated as the second part of the proof of copying. Depending on the media of the work, you will make verbal, aural, visual, or more substantive comparisons to see if the similarity is obvious. I recommend that you not proceed with a lawsuit unless the similarity is obvious to a disinterested observer, which the judge certainly will be if you take the case to court. The trial judge most likely will evaluate this form of substantial similarity as proof of copying at the motion to dismiss or summary judgment stage, and will be informed by the briefs and submissions of counsel, but guided by her own eyes and ears. What is obvious or plain to perceive is most definitely in the eye or ear of the beholder, so pass your evidence around to more than a few eyes or ears to determine if you have the right stuff. You and your client are not impartial in this determination.

Step Five: Make a Demand

The choice to put this step as number five on the list is a bit arbitrary. Deciding to make a demand is a choice that should take place after you are fairly certain that you or your client has a viable copyright infringement claim, and that can come before or after you have expended a lot of time verifying all of the steps of the dispute listed here. Therefore, consider this "step five" label to be "make a demand when you are comfortable with the merits of the claim."

It is true that in most intellectual property disputes, the owner of the right (i.e., the copyright owner) generally calls out the alleged copyist by making a demand to cease and desist copying. The tone and specifics of such a demand is up to you (and your lawyer, if you are not the lawyer). Sometimes an early demand is a cordial invitation to work out the situation, as seen in this demand letter by Jack Daniel's counsel regarding a trademark dispute, available at https://brokenpianoforpresident.files.wordpress.com/2012/07/jd-letter-entire-big1.jpg; *see also* http://www.abajournal.com/news/article/jack_daniels_cease-and-desist_letter_goes_viral_for_being_exceeedingly_poli/. And sometimes your demand will be more forceful.

Hopefully, you will resolve the dispute at this stage, and, in truth, many disputes do go away at this stage because the costs of moving forward are high for both the copyright owner and the alleged copyist. But if your initial demands or proposals fall on deaf ears with the alleged copyist, then you must move on to the next steps.

Step Six: Form Your Allegations Regarding the Elements of Infringement

At step six, you are contemplating an actual lawsuit in which you will need to allege the infringement claim itself. The elements of a copyright infringement claim that must be alleged in a complaint are:

- A copying

- of a "substantial and material" portion

- of protected elements of plaintiff's work

- producing a work that is substantially similar to plaintiff's work

Substantial and Material vs. De Minimis

Plaintiff must establish that a "substantial and material portion" of the protected elements of plaintiff's work was copied. Substantial and material means more than trivial, more than a de minimis portion, but not necessarily the whole work.

Copyists cannot defend themselves in an infringement suit by pointing out that they could have copied a lot more of plaintiff's work, but didn't. As the wise old Circuit Judge Learned Hand said in *Sheldon v. Metro-Goldwyn Pictures Corp.*,[2] the **"Pirate cannot defend a taking but pointing out how much more he could have stolen."**

A substantial and material portion means something **more than trivial**. There is a **de minimis** standard that applies to determine whether the copying is something so small, so trivial, that the court will not spend its time thinking about it. The actual legal phrase in Latin that applies here is, *de minimis non curat lex*, translated as "The law does not concern itself with trifles."

First, remember the potency of the derivative works right. Plaintiff, the copyright owner, has the right to authorize, control, or prevent any work based upon one or more of his preexisting works, such as a translation, musical arrangement, dramatization, art reproduction, **or any other form** in which the work may be recast, transformed, or adapted.

Derivative works need not incorporate most of the original work or even the "heart" of the work—it potentially infringes the owner's rights if the second work incorporates **a *portion*** of the copyrighted work **in some form**. Examples of this doctrine in practice are:

- *Campbell v. Acuff Rose Music*—2 Live Crew took the opening lines of Roy Orbison's "Oh, Pretty Woman" song and his bass riff, and repeated the theme throughout the parody; it was held to be substantial and material, not de minimis.[3]

- *Harper & Row v. Nation Enters.*—Nation took 300 words of verbatim quotes from Ford's memoirs, but it was considered by the court to be the most interesting and important part of the memoirs; it was held to be substantial and material, not de minimis.[4]

- *Los Angeles News Service* "Beating of Reginald Denny" Tape Cases—In actions against CBS, Reuters Television, and KCAL-TV, courts held that using a few seconds of a 4 minute 30 second videotape could be infringement; in each case it was held to be substantial and material, not de minimis.[5]

- *Bridgeport Music* Cases—Using just a few seconds of a sound recording and incorporating just a few notes or words into a new recording still can be infringement. The courts in each of the *Bridgeport Music* cases practically guaranteed that no matter how small the portion was, it would not be found to be trivial, because the courts held that if the defendant thought the portion it took was worthwhile to copy, loop, or mash-up, then that little bit must be substantial and material, not de minimis.[6]

De Minimis Use

Ringgold v. Black Entertainment Television (1997)[7]

In *Ringgold*, the artist, Faith Ringgold, had created a story quilt that was part of the collection of the High Museum of Art in Atlanta, and the museum had issued and sold a poster of the quilt.[8] This poster wound up as set decoration on the Black Entertainment Television (BET) program, *Roc*. In the episode discussed in the opinion, the poster of the story quilt was placed in a part of the set that was used frequently for conversations between the major characters of the episode. The poster and the quilt were seen several times in the episode, but only for a few seconds each time.

Ringgold Story Quilt Poster

The court applied the following factors to determine if the use was de minimis:

- Amount used

- Time of exposure

- Prominence—focus, lighting, camera angles

The quilt poster was seen in its entirety, and was on air for a total of 27 seconds of air time—but again, each showing was a few seconds in length, and the poster never was featured as the subject of full screen shot. The camera did not dwell on the poster or use it in the promotion of the episode; it was most often seen in the background of the action, behind characters, in slant angles and partial shots.

The court also applied a fourth factor—whether the practice of the television industry was to license the kind of exposure and prominence that was at issue in the case. In this, the defendant BET ran into some bad luck, because plaintiff Ringgold proved that the Library of Congress charges PBS rates for uses of images in full screen, partial screen, or partial shots of the work, including use in the background of scenes. Thus, someone at copyright central (the Library of Congress) thought this kind of use was worth paying for, and the court of appeals did not disagree. The court found it was not a de minimis use, and therefore it infringed on Ringgold's copyright.

Actual De Minimis Uses

Ringgold tells a cautionary tale, and the court wrote a thorough opinion that is likely to be quoted and applied for years to come, but the case is not the only one to take up the issues of incidental appearance de minimis claims:

- *Jackson v. Warner Bros.*—considered the use of two Earl Jackson works in the *Made in America* movie. As in *Ringgold*, the works were hanging on the wall of one set in the movie, and got the most screen time in a scene in which the two main characters, played by Whoopie Goldberg and Ted Danson, had a fumbling, groping romantic embrace in which they actually bumped into one of the pictures and set it askew. Nevertheless, the court found the use to be de minimis.[9]

- *Leicester v. Warner Bros.*—considered the use of a sculpture in the *Batman Forever* movie. The work was held to be part of the architectural features of an existing bank building, and declared that it is okay to copy and use architectural features of building that are observable from the street. The sculpture later was adapted and transformed to become the International Bank of Gotham in the movie.[10]

Copying in a Different Media

The derivative works standard fully embraces the concept of a copy that is rendered in a different media than the original. Copying an artistic design into another medium is not a protected use. Going from a drawing to a sculpture or from a photograph to a painting or sculpture is not allowed. In this way, 3-dimensional copies can infringe on 2-dimensional images, patterns, and designs, and vice versa, 2-dimensional pictures or photographs can violate the copyright of a 3-dimensional sculpture.

- *Jones Bros v. Underkoffler*—3-D gravesite memorial violated the copyright over a 2-D design drawing of gravesite memorials.[11]

- *King Features Synd. v. Fleischer*—3-D toy based on 2-D "Sparkplug" character from Barney Google cartoon violated the cartoon's copyright.[12]

- *Fleischer Studios v. Ralph A. Freundlich*—3-D "Betty Boop" doll violated the copyright over the 2-D Betty Boop cartoon.[13]

- *Gaylord v. United States*—2-D photograph featured on a postage stamp violated the copyright over the 3-D Korean War Memorial sculpture.[14]

Substantial Similarity in the Infringement Analysis

The substantial similarity analysis at the infringement stage is a little more complicated than the test of the same name at the "proof of copying" stage. Most "proof of copying" substantial similarity analyses can be done by the trial judge simply by examining the two works side-by-side. If the two works look or sound similar, they are similar. At the infringement stage, the law is more rigorous and requires more facts (more evidence and testimony), and often requires the input of experts.

For infringement claims, there are two tests for substantial similarity:

- **Extrinsic Similarity**—Asks the jury to consider the general similarity of the protected elements of the two works: Do they have similar features? Do they look (sound, feel) the same?

- **Intrinsic Similarity**—Asks if an average viewer would appreciate the value and expression of the two works the same; would the average viewer weigh the desirable artistic merits of the two works as the same; would this viewer assume that one work was based on the other?

Expert testimony is available on **extrinsic** features, but **not** on **intrinsic** similarity. In other words, the expert witness can instruct the jury to see and hear things with a more educated eye or ear—for example, she could testify to the jury, "You may not notice this, but the brush strokes here are very similar . . ." or "This passage repeats the passage of music from movement 1 of plaintiff's work. If you listen closely, the drumming pattern is the same . . ."—but she cannot tell the jury how to appreciate the merits of the two works, nor whether one substitutes for the other or seems to be an extension of the other.

Step Seven: Does the Defendant Have a Fair Use Defense?

We have come a long way toward establishing the bases for the owner's lawsuit, but a good copyright owner or lawyer will anticipate the defenses that the copyist is likely to raise. At the end of the day, the owner can fight the fight through all the steps of the action, all the way to proving infringement, and the defendant still can escape liability by proving a fair use defense. That is how the First Amendment protects expressive uses that benefit the public and balances them against the monopoly rights of copyright. Fortunately, we covered this exact topic in Chapter 9, and the fair use doctrine and requirements will not be repeated here.

---

[1]   As in previous chapters, this chapter draws from the lessons of my prior work, particularly 1 LEONARD DUBOFF, MICHAEL D. MURRAY ET AL., ART LAW DESKBOOK: ARTISTS' RIGHTS IN INTELLECTUAL PROPERTY, MORAL RIGHTS, AND FREEDOM OF EXPRESSION 1-107–1-115 (2017).

[2]   *Sheldon v. Metro-Goldwyn Pictures Corp.*, 81 F.2d 49, 56 (2d Cir. 1936).

[3]   *Campbell*, 510 U.S. at 579-83.

[4]   *Harper & Row*, 471 U.S. at 539.

[5]   *LA News Serv.-CBS*, 305 F.3d at 929; *LA News Serv.-Reuters*, 149 F.3d at 993; *LA News Serv.-KCAL-TV*, 108 F.3d at 1120.

[6]   *Bridgeport Music-Dimension Films*, 383 F.3d at 399.

[7]   *Ringgold v. Black Entm't Television, Inc.*, 126 F.3d 70 (2d Cir. 1997).

[8]   Image: Michael D. Murray, Thumbnail-Sized Excerpt of Story Quilt Poster at Issue in the Lawsuit of *Ringgold v. Black Entm't Television, Inc.*, 126 F.3d 70, 80 (2d Cir. 1997).

[9]   *Jackson v. Warner Bros., Inc.*, 993 F. Supp. 585, 588-90 (E.D. Mich. 1997).

[10] *Leicester v. Warner Bros.*, 232 F.3d 1212, 1217-18 (9th Cir. 2000).

[11] *Jones Bros. Co. v. Underkoffler*, 16 F. Supp. 729 (M.D. Pa. 1936).

[12] *King Features Syndicate v. Fleischer*, 299 F. 533, 535-37 (2d Cir. 1924).

[13] *Fleischer Studios v. Ralph A. Freundlich, Inc.*, 5 F. Supp. 808 (S.D.N.Y. 1934).

[14] *Gaylord v. United States*, 595 F.3d 1364 (Fed. Cir. 2010).